PRIVATE GAME RESERVE

ENCOUNTERED

RESEARCHED, DEVELOPED AND CREATED
BY ULUSABA AND JACANA

Dear Geoffrey & Susan

"Never does Nature say one thing and Wisdom another..."

Warm Wishes

The Ulusaba Family

JACANA

Yellow-billed Kite
Milvus migrans
(55 cm) 126
This kite is a summer-breeding migrant from equatorial Africa. Its slightly forked, rudder-like tail is diagnostic in flight. It is highly manoeuvrable when gliding, and may rob other birds of their prey.

Sunset at Ulusa

FOREWORD

Africa – the mere mention of the word evokes visions of a vast, untamed continent filled with the adventure of rugged, harsh landscapes and abundant wildlife. It is a continent of contrasts and a melting pot rich in exciting cultures.

Economies throughout the continent are floundering, and many wildlife areas are teetering in the balance. The time has come, therefore, to realise that the scenic splendours of our flora an fauna have such massive drawing power that tourism, and particularly eco-tourism, remains the one industry that has almost unlimited potential. If correctly developed and managed, ou natural heritage could become our greatest industry, ensuring prosperity and employment fo much of the population.

Ulusaba is proud to be part of this initiative, not only to conserve a wilderness area and develop the local economy in South Africa, but also to educate and inform our visitors about the importance of local, and indeed global, conservation of our natural resources. This book, we believe, goes a long way to achieving this goal, and once taken home, could become a showcase filled with memories of our incredible wildlife spectacle. But more than that, we would hope that this wonderful place could become a retreat to be enjoyed with friends and family on countless occasions. It is a dynamic environment, forever changing, with every visit guaranteed to be filled with exciting encounters at your home in Africa – Ulusaba.

Ulusaba
PRIVATE GAME RESERVE

Contents

Lowveld Yellow (page 11)

Natal Acraea (page 5)

Lowveld and Ulusaba

Ulusaba lies within the Lowveld, which is a broad, normally arid plain. The Lowveld's altitude ranges from 150 to 600 metres above sea level. It stretches between the Lebombo mountains in the east, bordering Mozambique, and the Drakensberg escarpment in the west. The plain is a savannah, which is grassland covered with sparse to dense bush. The Lowveld is dissected by several rivers, which wind their way eastward towards the Indian Ocean.

Rainfall varies between 200 and 600 mm per year, decreasing from west to east and from south to north. Most of the rain falls during summer in the form of thunderstorms. Summers are hot and humid, with temperatures frequently exceeding 35°C. Winters are warm, and night-time temperatures seldom fall to freezing point. As the Lowveld is a relatively arid zone, rainfall is one of the most important factors influencing this ecosystem. At the end of the dry winter, the first substantial summer rains bring new life to the bush.

An unusual early morning view of both Rock and Safari Lodges, Ulusaba

An Overview

The geology and climate in any area create both the types and the variety of habitats found there. The habitats in turn determine which plant and animal species will thrive in the area. Ulusaba and the Lowveld, therefore, consist of their own particular group of habitats with their specific inhabitants. While some animals and plants prefer one particular habitat, others enjoy a wider range of environments. A very good rule for spotting any species – plant or animal – is to look for it where it thrives best.

The Buffalo-thorn Jujube an example of a plant th discourages feeding (page 6

Evolution

Plants have had to defend themselves against plant-eating (herbivorous) animals by evolving various ways of discouraging feeding. Some have developed thorns, while others secrete chemicals, that obstruct or reduce excessive feeding on any single plant.

Animal predators and their prey have also evolved together. They have both developed behavioural strategies that optimise their chances of survival.

Fire is another important factor influencing the environment. Plants and animals have adapted over tim to its presence. Many depend on fire for long-term survival. Whether natural or man-made, fires play an integral role in maintaining the Lowveld ecosystem.

Examples of animals' means of defence: Porcupine quills (page 59) and Leopard Tortoise shell (page 30)

A klipspringer (page 24), poised on top of a granite outcrop, uses the height to watch for preda and gain a high haven of relative saf

Cheetah (page 21) use the flat, open spaces of a gabbro plain for successful hunting.

Sample of gabbro

Geology

The Lowveld can be roughly divided longitudinally into two main geological zones. In the west there are very old granites interspersed with areas of gabbro. Younger ecca shales, basalt and rhyolites are found in the east. Other than a few areas of gabbro, the main geological formations of Ulusaba are the ancient granite rocks. They are more than 3 500 million years old, and are the oldest part of the Earth's crust.

Granite is recognised by its light colour and formation: it erodes slowly (through wind and water) to form the gently rolling crests and valleys that characterise the Western Lowveld. Many rivers and drainage lines cut though them. In some places granite koppies or rocky hills with balancing boulders and domes of peeling rock remain as dominant landscape features. A variety of other soft minerals run like veins in the granite, and form lines of weakness along which the boulders break. Granite domes are created when the rocks are subject to repeated heating and cooling. Small cracks form, which are penetrated by water, causing layers of rock to peel off.

Erosion of the granite shield can be clearly seen at King's Rocks where the different blocks and layers are obvious. When standing on a granite boulder, think of the fact that the rocks at your feet are more than 3 500 million years old. These are amongst the oldest rocks known. There are few areas in the world where you are so close to the Earth's origins.

The black rocks near King's Rocks at Ulusaba are gabbro. They were formed about two hundred million years ago by magma pushing into long, line-like cracks in the ancient granite crust. The black rocks were exposed when this granite layer weathered away. Gabbro erodes rapidly to form landscapes consisting of flat plains. Here there are only a few drainage lines, and these often drain into seasonal pans.

The granite and gabbro rocks produce different soils. As a result, different groups of plants and animals thrive in each area.

Sample of granite

Map of Ulusaba

The most commonly used roads are depicted on the map, along with popular watering points and interesting landmarks. The road network affords access to a wide variety of habitats. This improves the chances of seeing the broad spectrum of the fauna and flora that this diverse region has to offer. The rangers and their trackers will ensure that each drive is a unique adventure!

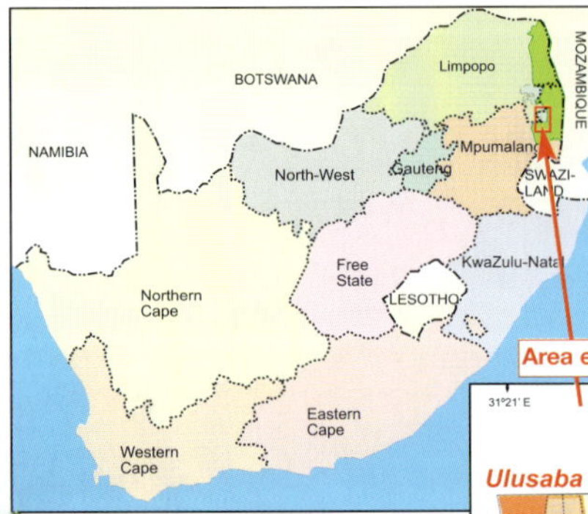

Map of South Africa showin[g] position of Ulusaba.

Enlarged area of Sabi San[d] showing Kruger National Park entrance gate

Weeping Bushwillow, Combretum collinum subsp. suluense (up to 15 m) 541.2 This tree usually grows on rocky or hilly slopes. It was named after Collina, the Greek goddess of the hillsides in classical mythology.

Ulusaba guests enjoying their surroundi[ngs]

Weeping Bushwillow flowers

ULUSABA

Ulusaba forms a part of the Sabi Sand Game Reserve in the Lowveld (see map, page vii). There are no fences between Ulusaba, Sabi Sand and the Kruger National Park. The fences were removed in 1993 to allow greater movement of game. Any animals seen on Ulusaba may roam all the way to the Lebombo mountains, bordering on Mozambique. These mountains lie 60 km to the east, forming the eastern boundary of the Kruger National Park.

Rock Lodge and Safari Lodge

The row of black, boulder-strewn hills on which Rock Lodge is built was formed millions of years ago. These hills stretch in a band between Bushbuckridge to the north-west and Skukuza to the south-east. Rock Lodg is about 560 metres above sea level, and is the highest lodge in the area. The spectacular view is unique in the Lowveld.

Special species seen at Ulusaba, African Crowned and Long-crested Eagles, the African Wood-Owl, and the aardwolf, are not frequently seen in the Lowveld. Being unusual they are exciting to find.

Long-crested Eagle
Lophaetus occipitalis
(53 - 58 cm) 139

African Crowned Eagle
Stephanoaetus coronatus
(80 - 90 cm) 141

These two eagles favour habitats with tall trees, such as forests, woodlands and plantations. The Long-crested Eagle is usually spotted perching on a high, dead tree with its conspicuous, long, floppy crest. The powerful African Crowned Eagle is more likely to be heard first, as it calls frequently across the forest.

Safari Lodge

Sunrise over the rolling hills of Ulusaba

Aardwolf
Proteles cristatus (H: 50 cm; 8,5 kg)
Preferring more open areas, nocturnal aardwolf mostly forage alone, and prey specifically on Harvester Termites. They dig their own burrows, or use old aardvark burrows for dens. The long mane of hair is raised erect at times of excitement or aggression.

olling Hills

ne dominant features of the landscape in the Ulusaba area are the rolling granite hills made up of crests and lleys. The erosion of granite has left coarse, unfertile sands on the crests. Rainwater seeps downhill through the nd, carrying leaves and other debris, as well as clay particles, into the valleys. This leaves the soils on the crests ss fertile, while soils in the valleys are constantly ch. The difference in conditions influences the pes of plants and animals that occur.

eplines are formed when water runs wnhill towards the valleys. However, on aching bedrock, it seeps to the surface again. is often occurs in the middle of the slope. ere a type of seepline habitat is formed, often cognisable by the mini-forests of Silver uster-leaf trees (page 3).

sides the rolling hills, Ulusaba consists of a variety of her habitats. These include rivers, drainage lines and pans; en areas and brackish sites; and rocky hills and termite ounds (pages xii - xvii).

African Wood-Owl
Strix woodfordii
(30 - 36 cm) 394
The seldom-seen Wood Owl breeds at the Safari Lodge, and its lovely hooting call can be heard at night.

Ulusaba

Crests & Valleys

The gently rolling granite hills create a variety of habitats for plants and animals. It is fascinating to understand how the landshape, geology and soils influence the flow of water and nutrients; how these influence the plants and their food content; and how the animals in turn influence the evolution of defence mechanisms found in the plants.

Humankind has become more aware of the important role the ecosystem plays in supplying our basic needs such as clean air and water. Conservation areas such as Ulusaba play an important role in conserving our natural resources.

Sunrise over a cre

Checklist for Crests and Valleys

pg.	**Mammals**
25	Bushbuck
25	Common Duiker
18	Giraffe
25	Kudu

(These landscapes are the choice of browsers)

	Birds
38	Burchell's Starling
36	Crested Barbet
38	Glossy Starling
37	Red-billed Buffalo Weaver
39	Red-billed Hornbill
39	Yellow-billed Hornbill

Crests

Rain water seeps through the coarse unfertile soils of the crests. It is like a very "thin soup", providing little nourishment to the trees growing there. The trees therefore take in relatively large amounts of water to obtain enough nourishment for growth. Excess water, however, needs to be eliminated. The trees therefore have large leaves for water loss into the atmosphere.

Being low in nutrients, the leaves are not the first choice of browsers, but are still eaten at certain times. These trees defend themselves by producing chemicals that deter browsers (page 4).

Broad-leaved trees thrive on the crests, as they are adapted to grow in nutrient-poor, well-drained, sandy soils.

An example of a broad-leaved tree of the crests: Round-leaved Bloodwood (page 5).

Valleys

The finer particles of erosion, and plant and animal waste, are washed into the valleys to form richer soils. The water binds with the clay soil, and is not readily available to the plant roots. The result is soil low in water and high in nutrients. It is more like a "thick stew" compared to the "thin soup" of the crests.

The trees, therefore, have small, or fine, leaves to reduce water loss, such as those of Acacias. Grasses and trees occurring here are more palatable. As a result, more animals are found in the valleys.

Because they are sought after by browsers, valley trees have developed strong defence mechanisms such as growing thorns and/or secreting chemicals to reduce the feeding rate (pages 4 and 6).

Fine-leaved trees thrive in the valleys, as they are adapted to grow in nutrient-rich, clay soils that hold water.

n xample of fine- aved tree ith iorns: 'mbrella cacia (page 7)

Kiaat Bloodwood (Wild Teak) Pterocarpus angolensis (5 - 15 m) 236 This tree is found in both the crests and valleys of higher rainfall areas (more than 500 mm per year). The plate-winged, spiky pods are distinctive and conspicuous (February to August).

A typical valley as seen in Ulusaba

ULUSABA

WATER

Most animals are dependent on water. Rivers, drainage lines and pans, boreholes and dams provide different sources of water for the animals. Therefore the distribution of water affects the distribution of animals. This is especially true during winter, when rivers are low or dry, and seasonal pans dry up, forming muddy scars.

River pebbles

Rivers and Drainage Lines

The rivers of the Lowveld form snaking oases in an often-dry landscape. The Sand River is the largest river running through Ulusaba. Water use upstream, however, has decreased the river's flow significantly in winter. So although perennial, the river stops flowing completely during dry years. As a result, only a few deep pools are left in the river to provide water for the animals. The water still available under the sand provides essential nourishment to the riverine trees. If water is very scarce during the dry season, some animals such as elephant and warthog may dig in the dry riverbeds to quench their thirst.

The smaller drainage lines that run into the Sand River provide an invaluable water source. They create small perennial pools where water birds, reptiles, amphibians and fish can survive the dry season.

Riverine vegetation provides essential shelter and food for many of the shyer animals. Elephant and buffalo use the shade of the trees to rest during hotter times of the day.

Checklist for River and Drainage Lines

pg.	**Trees**
10	Ebony Jackal-berry
3	Leadwood
11	Sycomore Fig
	(These are the largest trees found along the river)
	Mammals
19	Buffalo
25	Bushbuck
19	Elephant
21	Leopard
25	Nyala
22	Waterbuck
	Birds
46	Burchell's Coucal
61	Giant Eagle Owl
44	Green Pigeon
46	Orange-breasted Bush Shrike
46	Paradise Flycatcher
45	Purple-crested Lourie
46	Southern Boubou Shrike
44	Trumpeter Hornbill

Elephants (page 19) washing in the Sand River

African Jacana (page 49), a bird that favours slow-moving water where lily pads provide a unique habitat base.

River Bushwillow
Combretum erythrophylum
(5 - 12 m) 536
This tree is only found along permanent rivers where it may grow in ense stands. It has typical ombretum four-winged pods, hich are small and often bundant. It is not very alatable, but giraffe and ephant eat its leaves.

Elephants (page 19) drinking from the Pumphouse Pan

Checklist for Open Pans

pg.	Trees
xiii	Flaky-bark Acacia
9	Magic Guarri (dense stands)
	Mammals
19	Elephant
21	Leopard
21	Lion
22	Warthog
18	White Rhino
	Reptiles & Amphibians
33	Grey Tree Frog
33	Terrapins
	Birds
49	African Pied Wagtail
48	Blacksmith Plover
50	Egyptian Goose
48	Hamerkop
51	Saddle-billed Stork
60	Water Dikkop

Open Water: Pans

Many pans are natural depressions, often found in brackish areas (see page xiv). During the rainy season, animals such as rhino and warthog wallow in muddy patches, creating hollows in the clay soil. These fill up with water after rain and form the pans. The pans make it possible for animals to spread out in summer, away from permanent water and away from high predator concentrations. This gives the vegetation around permanent water a chance to recover.

Ulusaba rangers and management are sensitive to the environment, which they manage with care. Trees such as the Round-leaved Bloodwood (page 5) sometimes obscure the view of visitors. These trees are, however, a favourite of elephant, and are not removed.

Flaky-bark Acacia
Acacia exuvialis
(2 - 5 m) 164.1
The small Flaky-bark Acacia is first recognised by its typical, feathery Acacia leaves. Its smooth bark, which peels in large, orange-brown flakes, leaving a smooth, yellow-brown under-surface is characteristic.

Ulusaba

Open Areas

Open areas have fewer trees and therefore more grass. They are very important for grazing species that need an abundance of different grasses. Many of these animals occur in large herds. They need not only the grasses as food, but also the visibility of unwooded areas to be able to detect threatening predators.

Open areas are ideal for animal photography. To ensure the animals are comfortable enough for close-up photography to be possible, they must be treated with respect. Only a few vehicles are allowed near the animals, and noise levels and movement must be kept to a minimum.

Pan and brackish site along the Mabrak River

Plains Ze(bra)
(page 23)

Checklist for Open Areas

pg.	**Mammals**
23	Blue Wildebeest
21	Cheetah
23	Plains Zebra
18	White Rhino
	Birds
37	Ground Hornbill
37	Helmeted Guineafowl
37	Red-crested Korhaan

Checklist for Brackish Sites

	Birds
60	Bronze-winged Courser
36	Crowned Plover

Checklist for Clearings and Burnt Areas

	Trees
9	Jacket-plum
9	Magic Guarri
9	Umvala Gardenia

Brackish Sites

Over millennia, flood waters deposit layers of silt along the rivers and drainage lines of granite landscapes. These soils are high in salts and create flat, open patches called brackish flats. The vegetation growing here tolerates these salty soils, and there are numerous open areas of short grass. The grasses are very palatable, and are usually heavily grazed, leaving bare patches of exposed soil.

Clearings

Apart from the brackish sites, the bush in Ulusaba is normally fairly dense. It is therefore not suitable for animals that like open areas. When Ulusaba managemen(t) clears the bush, animals needing open areas can move in. The cheetah (a threatened species), specialised to hunt i(n) open areas, can then extend its home range.

Bush encroachment occurred on Ulusaba as a result of past management practices. Management therefore clea(rs) certain areas of this bush to improve veld condition.

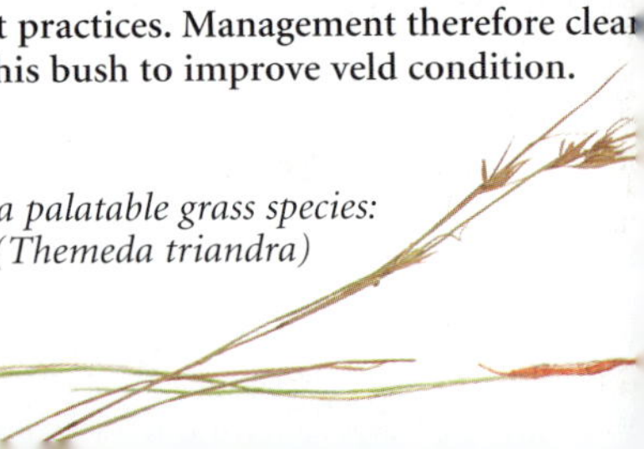

An example of a palatable grass species: Rooigras/Red Grass (Themeda triandra)

Lions (page 21) resting in shade in a clearing

Burnt Areas

Recently burnt areas are very attractive to all grazers, as the new green flush of vegetation is very tasty and rich in nutrients. Species such as zebra, wildebeest and even White Rhino often move in to feed on new, exposed, green shoots. Zebra eat these new shoots while the grass is still smouldering.

Cheetahs (page 21), on a burnt termite mound, use the height to look for prey that are feeding on new grass.

ULUSABA

ROCKY HILLS AND TERMITE MOUNDS

Rocky hills and termite mounds are further examples of the fascinating variety of habitats that occur on Ulusaba. They create a unique set of environmental conditions, and particular groups of plant and animal species thrive in these specific environments.

View from Rock Lodge looking westward over rocky hills

Large-leaved Rock Fig
Ficus abutifolia
(6 m) 63

The Large-leaved Rock Fig only grows over rocks. Its roots grow deep into the crevices in search of water and nutrients. The roots help split the rocks and aid weathering.

Rocky Hills

Granite rocks form the rocky hills or koppies seen in the Ulusaba area. Water and nutrient-rich soils collect in the crevices of the rocks, and the rocky boulders also provide protection and shade. As a result lusher vegetation grows here, and many plants and animals are better adapted to live in this environment. Leopards often use the hills to hide and rest during the day. Baboons use the boulders as vantage points to keep a look-out for enemies. The klipspringer, suited for climbing and jumping, could not survive in open areas where running speed is needed to escape predators.

Mocking Cliff-Cha
Thamnolae
cinnamomeiventr
(22 cm) 59

The Mocking Chat inhabit rocky areas, usually in group of 4 - 5 birds. When landin from flight, it conspicuousl raises and lowers its tai

Checklist for Rocky Hills

pg.	**Trees**
xvi	Large-leaved Rock Fig
xvi	Resurrection Bush
	Mammals
27	Baboon
24	Klipspringer
21	Leopard
	Reptiles
31	Giant Plated Lizard
	Birds
xvi	Mocking Chat

Resurrection Bush
Myrothamnus flabellifolius
(20 - 40 cm)

A small erect bush growing on rocky surfaces. During winter, it is dried-out and looks dead, but revives within hours after rain.

Termite Mounds (Termitaria)

These large mounds are mainly the dwellings of the termite *Macrotermes natalensis*. More than half the mounds seen are active. When a mound is damaged the worker and soldier termites appear within minutes to start the repair work.

The soils of the termitaria are very fertile, and seeds dropped here germinate and grow easily. As soon as one tree grows, birds rest there, depositing more seeds on the mound. Gradually a small forest develops, often including the Ebony Jackal-berry and Weeping Boer-bean (page 10), as well as palatable grasses such as Blue Buffalo Grass. Many animals use old mounds as dens or homes.

Lioness (page 21) on a termite mound

Checklist for Termite Mounds

Animals whose life-cycles are associated with Termite Mounds:

pg.	**Mammals**
59	Aardvark
27	Dwarf Mongoose
21	Hyaena
59	Pangolin
59	Porcupine
22	Warthog
20	Wild Dog
	Reptiles
31	Rock Monitor
31	Southern African Python

Blue Buffalo Grass
Cenchrus ciliaris
(up to 1,5 m)

Termites, Macrotermes natalensis
(25 mm; queen: 10 cm)
Widespread, these large termites cultivate fungus within the warm, humid termitaria to feed their young. They recycle humus and dead wood, but are also well known wood destroyers.

Seasons and Stars

As each year passes, variations in temperature and rainfall transform the environment season by season. Seemingly lifeless vegetation springs to life, rivers of water become sand, and creatures of every size, shape and colour battle the elements and each other in the eternal fight for survival. At night the sky reveals a continual parade of celestial wonders, each with its own story to tell. A good time to view these constellations is within an hour of sunset. Using the Meade 12-inch LX200 telescope, and guided by the expert knowledge of Ulusaba rangers, stargazers can discover more than 64 000 of the most spectacular "jewels" of the cosmos.

During game drives and walks the changes of the seasons are often highlighted by the presence of young mammals. Some are year-round regulars, while others are seasonal specialists.

Breeding Season: All year round
January to December

Black Rhino p. 18
Chacma Baboon p. 27
Common Duiker p. 25
Elephant p. 19
Giraffe p. 18
Hippo p. 19
Hyaena p. 21
Leopard p. 21
Lion p. 21
Nyala p. 25
Vervet Monkey p. 26
White Rhino p. 18

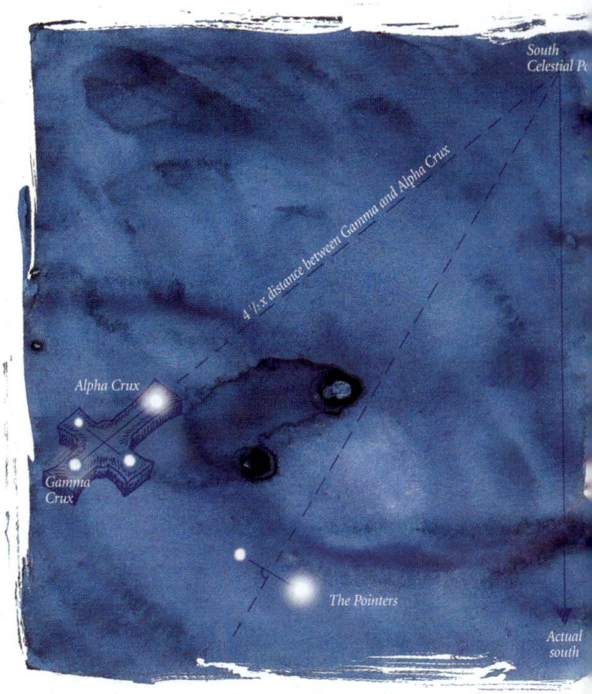

The Southern Cross can help you find the South Celestial Pole

The Southern Cross

The Southern Cross, or Crux, is the best-known constellation in the southern sky. It is at its highest point in June. It can give you various kinds of information.

1. To find the South Celestial Pole
Use either of these two ways:

- Draw an imaginary line through the long axis of the Southern Cross, and extend it into space. Then, from mid-way between the pointers, draw a perpendicular line into space. Where the lines cross is roughly the South Celestial Pole, or South Pole in the sky.
- Measure the space between the two stars (Gamma Crux and Alpha Crux) that form the long axis of the cross. Then measure a distance beyond Alpha Crux of four-and-a-half times the space between the two stars. This is roughly the position of the South Celestial Pole.

2. To work out latitude
Measure the degrees between the horizon and the celesti pole to find out at what latitude you are. Line up the bas of a protractor on the horizon. This must be a level horizon, not on hills or mountains. Now read the numbe of degrees to the South Celestial Pole.

To tell the time of night
ɔpy this sketch, and
ɪt it into the shape
ˈ a disc.

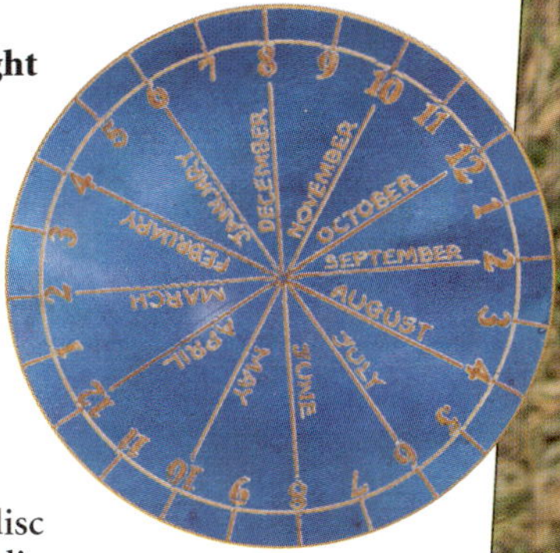

Iold the disc with he line of the urrent month ɔointing vertically ıpwards. (If the date is ːlose to the middle of he month, adjust the disc ·oughly by holding the line ɔetween the present month and the next month upright).

- Move the disc until the long axis of the Southern Cross points to its centre. Read the time of night shown by the long axis.

Remember that in the northern parts of South Africa the Southern Cross is sometimes not visible. At these times, obviously, the "watch" will not work.

Hyaena cubs are born all year round (page 21).

'hite Rhino (page 18) with calf – also a year-round breeder

Seasons and Stars

Spring (August to October)

The Milky Way is rising and is almost overhead by September. Early in the season Virgo, with its prominent alpha star Spica (the 16th-brightest star in our sky), can be seen setting in the west.

The spring is arguably the best season to visit the bush. The temperature is rising, there are no mosquitoes, and the lack of grass and absence of leaves from many trees makes spotting easier. Animals are concentrated around whatever water remains after the dry winter. As soon as there is even a sprinkling of rain, flowers appear, both on the ground and, spectacularly, on many of the trees. From September, migrant birds that have spent our winter in warmer areas return, to nest or simply to enjoy the good weather and the wealth of food that spring and summer bring.

Breeding Season: Spring
(increasing warmth and rain)

	Aug	Sep	Oct
Seasonal breeders			
Warthog *(Oct - Dec)* p. 22			■
Year-round breeders with seasonal peaks			
Bushbuck *(Oct - Dec)* p. 25			■
Cheetah *(Jul - Dec)* p. 21	■	■	■
Steenbok *(Sep - Oct)* p. 24		■	■
Waterbuck *(Oct)* p. 22			■

Summer Triangle

Aquila

Cygnus

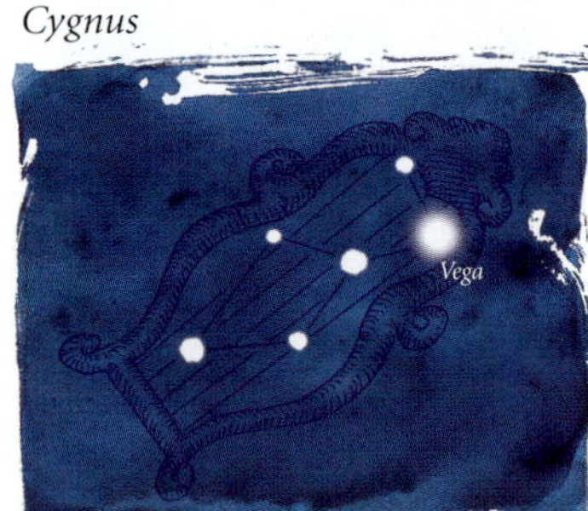

Lyra

Aquila, Cygnus and Lyra

September and early October are good times for viewing a group of three constellations that hold centre stage in the north. Aquila the Eagle, with its alpha star Altair, is in the central north. Cygnus the Swan, including Deneb (the 19th-brightest star), and Lyra the Harp with its alpha star Vega (the 5th-brightest), occupy positions on either side of Aquila, close to the northern horizon. The three alpha stars, Altair, Deneb and Vega, form the "Summer Triangle", although they are best seen in our spring. Cygnus, with Deneb at the tail, is flying north, and is also called the Northern Cross.

Violet (page 14)

Eastern Rhigozum (page 15)

Virgo contains over 200 galaxies, belonging to the Virgo Supercluster, of which our own Milky Way galaxy is a member. It is best observed just after sunset.

Blue-headed Tree Agama (page 30)

bra
little higher up and to the east Virgo is the kite-shaped bra – the "Scales". ptember is the best ne to see this nstellation.

Bushfire at Ulusaba

Shaving-brush ushwillow (page 12)

Aspects of Spring

At this stage of the year the build-up of tinder-dry combustible material creates a serious fire hazard. As temperatures increase and the spring winds blow, bush fires can ravage the land.

Reptiles and insects become active again, with butterflies being particularly conspicuous as they drink the nectar of the beautiful wers, shrubs and trees that dot the landscape. They turn the browny-yellow rroundings into a kaleidoscope of colour. Termite alates – "winged termites" – "flying ants" erupt in their thousands from termite ounds. The exact triggering mechanism, thought to be a lance of temperature and humidity, is little understood.

(M)

Guineafowl Butterfly
Hamanumida daedalus
(60 mm) Visible all year

Seasons and Stars

Summer (November to March)

November allows a peek at the northern skies, with the Great Square within Pegasus dominating the sky to the north. Fomalhaut (the 18th-brightest star in our night sky) is almost directly overhead. The Milky Way is setting in the south, with Altair (the 11th-brightest star) setting in the west (see page xx). As the constellations "move" westward across the sky, more "jewels" become visible, with Taurus well established by December.

Summer in Africa is generally a vibrant season, with the more-regular rains signalling a revival and rebirth of the land. The breeding season starts for most species, and the bush comes alive with sights, colours, displays and sounds, as creatures great and small compete to attract mates.

Pegasus
Unlike Leo, Pegasus is the right way up for southern hemisphere observers, which is surprising considering it was named by northern astrologers. Just to the left of the rear leg is the finest galaxy visible through telescopes, and our closest neighbour in the Virgo Supercluster, the beautiful spiral galaxy called Andromeda (not shown in illustration).

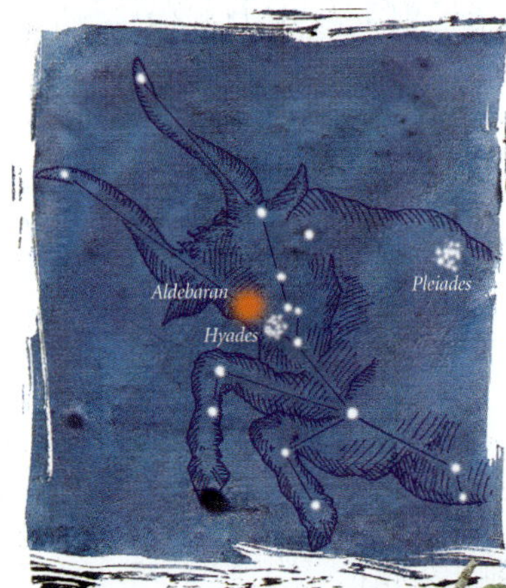

Taurus
This constellation i
dominated by the brilliant red star Aldebaran (the 13th-brightest star
Close by are the tw famous open clusters, the Hyade and the Pleiades ("Seven Sisters"). The latter is the easiest open cluster to see with the naked eye in the entire sky.

Breeding Season: Summer
(hot with rain)

Nov	Dec	Jan	Feb	Mar

Seasonal breeders

Blue Wildebeest	(Dec - Jan)	p. 23
Buffalo	(Jan - Apr)	p. 19
Impala	(Nov - Jan)	p. 24
Kudu	(Jan - Feb)	p. 25
Warthog	(Oct - Dec)	p. 22

Year-round breeders with seasonal peaks

Bushbuck	(Nov - Dec)	p. 25
Cheetah	(Jul - Dec)	p. 21
Common Reedbuck	(Dec - May)	p. 23
Plains Zebra	(Dec - Jan)	p. 23
Steenbok	(Mar - Apr)	p. 24
Waterbuck	(Feb - Mar)	p. 22

Sycomore Fig
(page 11)

River in summer flood

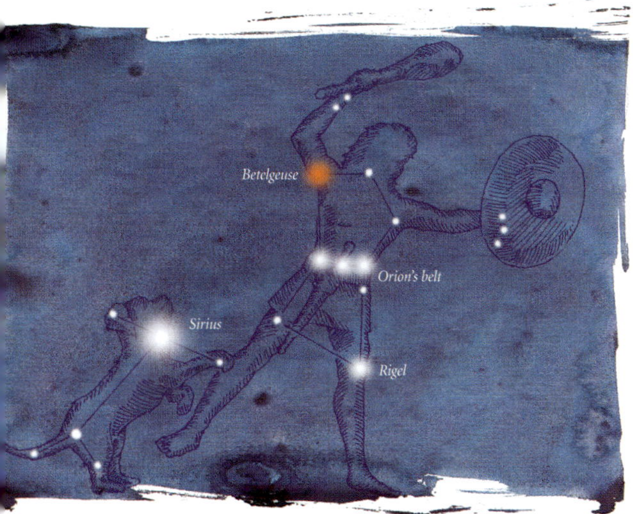

rion and Canis Major (looking south)
urus is followed by the famous hunter Orion and his big dog Canis Major, th being in prime viewing positions by January. Orion's "knee" to the west is e star called Rigel (the 7th-brightest star). It is estimated to be 57 000 times ighter than our Sun. Sirius, at 8,5 light years from Earth, is the brightest star the sky, and forms part of the head of Canis Major just east of Orion.

Gemini
The Gemini constellation (the "Twins", Castor and Pollux – 23rd- and 17th-brightest respectively) follows the hunting party, and is best placed for observation in March.

Aspects of Summer

Temperatures can rise into the id-40s, and humidity is generally gh in mid-to-late summer. The mmer rainfall season is aracterised by afternoon understorms with a lot of rain lling in relatively short periods. is causes the usually dry sand riverbeds d drainage lines to flow in torrential torrents ich last from a few minutes to many hours. is does wonders to raise the water table and rejuvenate erine vegetation, supplying juicy fruits to a host of species. Fish, crocodiles, frogs and terrapin, as well as various insects whose life cycles depend on water, all benefit from this phenomenon.

Ebony Jackal-berry (page 10)

Many birds, including raptors, return to the Lowveld in summer, some of them to breed. Wahlberg's Eagle is a breeding migrant.

Wahlberg's Eagle (page 52)

Thunderstorm over the Lowveld

Seasons and Stars

Autumn and Winter (April to July)

Autumn and winter are probably the best seasons for viewing the skies, and a host of constellations can be seen rising and setting over a four-month period. Three of the most interesting (Boötes, Scorpio and Leo) are represented here.

The season begins with Sirius (alpha star of Canis Major, page xxiii), Procyon (alpha star of Canis Minor, and 8th-brightest) and Canopus (2nd-brightest and approximately 80 000 times brighter than our Sun) dominating the entire sky near the meridian. The Milky Way passes between them from north to south. Taurus, Orion and Gemini are setting in the west and, by May, Leo is the dominant northern constellation.

June and July are best for viewing the creature that kills Orion the Hunter – Scorpio, the Scorpion. This is an extensive constellation that dominates the southern sky along with Crux, the Southern Cross (page xviii).

Winter is a time of clear blue skies, cool evenings and cool misty mornings, with spectacular sunsets and sunrises.

Boötes
Through May anc June the brilliant red star Arcturus (4th-brightest) is major attraction i the north as it heralds the arriva of Boötes, the "Bear Hunter". Ju above the norther horizon we are al very fortunate to glimpse the "Big Dipper", part of Ursa Major, the "Big Bear", which is best viewed in the northern hemisphere. It occupies the sky below and to the west of Boötes.

Combretum pods (page 5)

Breeding Season: Autumn & Winter
(cool and dry)

Apr	May	Jun	Jul

Seasonal breeders

Buffalo *(Jan - Apr) p. 19*

Wild Dog *(May - Jun) p. 20*

Year-round breeders with seasonal peaks

Bushbuck *(Apr - May) p. 25*

Cheetah *(Jul - Dec) p. 21*

Common Reedbuck *(Dec - May) p. 23*

Steenbok *(Mar - Apr) p. 24*

Tree de-barked by elephants

Leo
This is one of the few constellations that actually resembles the creature depicted in the legends. However, the lion in southern Africa is seen upside down in the sky. The constellation includes the "Sickle" – part of the head and mane of Leo – as well as more than 20 galaxies. The alpha star, Regulus (21st-brightest), is a red supergiant and is actually three stars, the two companions visible only through a large telescope.

Scorpio
The bright red supergiant and alpha star of Scorpio, Antares, is the 15th-brightest, and is so big that our entire solar system up to the orbit of Jupiter would fit into it. Antares means "rival to Mars". It is so brilliant and so red that it is often confused with this planet.

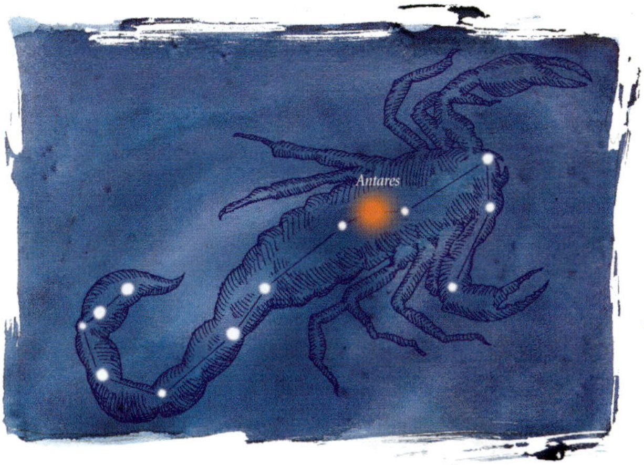

Rutting impala (page 24)

Aspects of Autumn and Winter

utumn to early winter rings the rutting of ntelope, and as it ecomes drier animals nd it more difficult to nd food. Insects and ptiles enter their ormant cycles, and igrant birds leave. nimals move into iet mode", eating ods and low-nutrient ods.

lephants play a major le in habitat anipulation as they e-bark trees for the utrients stored there. hey also dig in river beds get to water, which n be used by other nimals as well.

Cheetah (page 21)

Acacia pods (page 7)

Plants and Insects

Plants are closely linked to their environment, and reflect changes in climate and soil. This is because plants have evolved over millennia and adapt to specific soil, temperature and moisture conditions. Common plants found in the Lowveld are susceptible to frost, but can withstand the long, seasonal droughts.

The plants are also adapted to specific patterns of animal usage and to fire. The plants are all protected in some way against over-usage by browsing animals (page 6). Fire accelerates the breakdown of dead plant material, and encourages new growth.

Because plants provide essential food, nesting and sheltering sites, they determine the different kinds of mammals, birds, reptiles and insects found in an area.

Many insects have been included with the plants. They all use the plants in some way, and are also associated with certain habitats.

Sizes given refer to the height of average adult plants, to the wingspan of butterflies, and to the body length of other insects. All trees have been given their national tree numbers. Previous common tree names are given in brackets. The months given after the names of the flowering plants refer to the times they flower.

The spiky, protective outer shell of this Armoured Ground Cricket provides protection against most insectivores.

Trees

Trees can be identified in a number of ways: by their growth form, by the striking features of leaves, flowers, pods and/or bark, and by the type of habitat/s they prefer. By remembering one or two of the above features, you will learn to recognise common trees.

Striking and Common

Wherever you stop, you have a good chance of seeing at least one of the trees on this page. Each species has specific habitat preferences, but is more easily recognised by its striking features.

Every tree tells a story about the area in which it grows. By getting to know the trees, you can learn and understand more about the environment too.

◄ Apple-leaf ▲
Philenoptera violacea
(Lonchocarpus capassa)
Flowers: Oct - Nov
(5 - 18 m) 238
The irregularly shaped canopy, meandering trunk, and large, pale leaves that grow in groups of three, are all characteristic. It grows in most parts of the Lowveld, especially along rivers and streams, and most often in groups. Bunches of fragrant, purple flowers appear in summer.

◄ African Monarch (Milkweed Butterfly)
Danaus chrysippus aegyptius
(50 - 70 mm)
The caterpillars feed on the milkweed (Family *Asclepiadaceae*), which contain a toxic, milky latex. The adult butterflies retain this substance, and are poisonous to insect-eaters and are thus avoided. They occur in most habitats.

▲ Knob-thorn Acacia ►
Acacia nigrescens
(2 - 18 m) 178
These upright thorny trees can be identified by the conspicuous woody knobs along the trunks of young trees and larger branches. In early summer, spectacular masses of creamy-white flower spikes cover the canopy. Baboon, monkey and giraffe eat the flowers. White-backed Vultures (page 53) often nest on the tops of the trees.

Cicada ▼
Family *Cicadidae*
(20 mm)
The shrill call of male cicadas to attract females is often heard in the bush. They lie up against the trunks of trees, but perfect camouflage makes sightings very difficult.

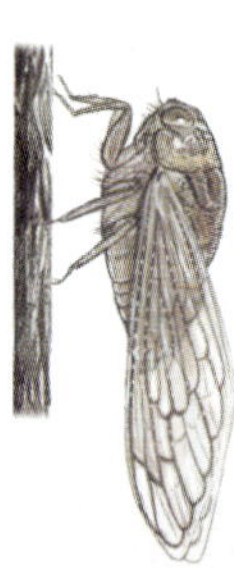

◄ Silver Cluster-leaf ►
Terminalia sericea
Pods: Jan - Jun (6 - 20 m) 551
This tree loves well-drained, sandy soils, and is often seen growing along seeplines. It is recognised by its horizontal branches with pale, shiny leaves covered with silver hairs. Two-winged pods appear from January to June. Elephant, giraffe, kudu and impala eat the leaves and young shoots.

◄ Marula
Sclerocarya birrea
Fruit: Nov - Mar (7 - 17 m) 360
The Marula can be identified by its trunk, marked by smooth pink-brown depressions lying within dark bark. The tasty fruit, often seen lying under female trees, is eaten by numerous animals, insects, birds, and humans. The fruit is used for various products, from jam to a very intoxicating beer.

The Marula is one of the most important indigenous fruit-bearing trees. Marula trees were planted by the early inhabitants over hundreds of years. Their presence often indicates the position of an old settlement.

▼ Leadwood Bushwillow ►
Combretum imberbe
Pods: Feb - May (20 m) 539
Characteristic features of Leadwood Bushwillow are the bark, which breaks up into small, pale-grey, regular blocks, like snake-skin, and small four-winged pods. It is common in the Lowveld in low-lying areas and near streams and rivers. As the tree's name implies, the wood is very hard. Dead trees decay very slowly, and often become well-known landmarks.

▼ Millipede
Class *Diplopoda*
(up to 20 cm)
Millipedes are scavengers and plant-eaters. They secrete chemicals, which give them a distinctive odour that keeps predators away. When disturbed they writhe, or roll themselves into tight spirals.

Trees

The Crests

Tree identification is much easier once you know which common trees you are likely to find in each habitat. The rolling hills of the Lowveld are made up of numerous crests and valleys. The soils of the crests are sandy, and poor in nutrients. Because the soils are infertile, many less palatable, broad-leaved trees grow there, and they tend to be lower in nutrients.

Although these trees are generally unpalatable, their young shoots are eaten in spring, and their dropped leaves are eaten in winter. Many of the broad-leaved trees protect themselves by producing various levels of unpleasant-tasting chemicals, such as tannins. Tannins limit the availability of proteins by forming unabsorbable compounds. Sometimes animals may be forced to eat these unpalatable plants that they normally avoid because no other food is available. Then, because of the high tannin levels, the animals may not absorb enough nutrients for survival.

◄ **Blister Beetle**
Family *Meloidae* (5 - 40 mm)

These **insects both have striking colouration** to warn predators of their effective defences. **Blister Beetles** are distasteful, deterring lizards and birds, and humans are well aware of the **Honey Bees'** sharp sting. Blister Beetle larvae feed on locust eggs in the soil, and adults eat flowers throughout the summer months. Honey Bees live in colonies of up to 50 000, and play a vital role in pollination.

◄ **Honey Bee** ►
Apis mellifera adansonii
(15 mm)

▼ **Citrus Swallowtail**
Princeps demodocus
(80 - 90 mm)
Males fly around the tops of koppies at midday. Dozens may be seen roosting on grass stems under trees. Their caterpillars feed on citrus trees, and can be a pest in farming areas.

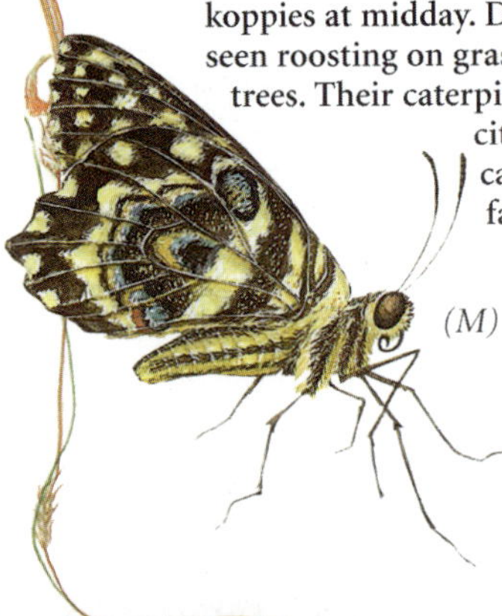

▼ **African Weeping-wattle** ▲
Peltophorum africanum
Flowers: Nov - Feb
(5 - 10 m) 215
The African Weeping-wattle has large, feathery leaves like those of Acacias. It prefers well-drained, sandy soils and is mostly unpalatable. The abundant yellow flowers are striking.

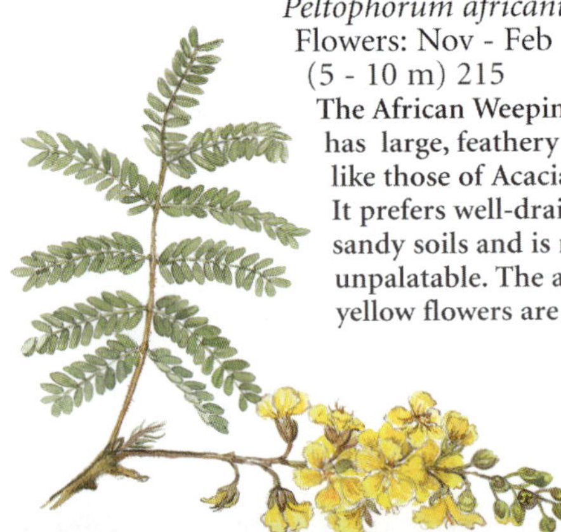

Natal Acraea ►
Acraea natalica natalica
(55 - 63 mm)
A very common butterfly, usually seen in the savannah areas, but it does spread into forest edges. It has an unusual zig-zag flight.

Bushwillows have inconspicuous flowers, but are recognised immediately by their four-winged pods, each species differing in size and colour. The **Red Bushwillow** has small pods (2,5 x 2 cm), green when young, turning reddish-brown when mature. The **Large-fruited Bushwillow**, as the name implies, has huge green pods (6 x 6 cm) which turn light-brown when ripe. The **Russet Bushwillow** also occurs in many other habitats besides the crests, and has small, brilliant, russet-red pods (2 x 2 cm), turning light-coppery-brown as they ripen.

ed Bushwillow
ombretum
iculatum
ods: Jan - May
- 10 m) 532

◄ Large-fruited Bushwillow
Combretum zeyheri
Pods: Feb - Oct
(5 - 15 m) 546

▲ Russet Bushwillow ►
Combretum hereroense
Pods: Jan - June
(3 - 5 m) 538

◄ Round-leaved Bloodwood ▼
(Round-leaved Teak)
Pterocarpus rotundifolius
Flowers: Sep - Feb (1 - 10 m) 237
The Round-leaved Bloodwood can grow into a tall tree, but in this area is usually seen as a multi-stemmed shrub, having been burnt back by fires. The large, glossy, round leaflets and yellow, pea-shaped flowers are characteristic features. Elephants are fond of the leaves and young twigs, and often break the tree.

◄ Antlion ▼ ►
Family *Myrmeleontidae*
(13 - 18 mm)
Groups of small conical pits, constructed by antlion larvae, are often seen in dry, sandy soil. They are traps for ants, on which the antlion larvae feed. The adults resemble dragonflies (page 48), except that the antennae of the adult antlion are conspicuous and club-like. When dragonflies rest, their wings are open, while antlion close theirs over their backs.

Larvae

Trees

The Valleys

The vegetation pattern of broad-leaved trees on the crests, and palatable fine-leaved trees in the valleys, can be seen in many of the undulating areas of South Africa. Trees of the valleys are mostly palatable and nutritious, because of the rich, fertile soils in which they grow. They are fine-leaved, and are actively sought by browsing animals. As a result, the trees have had to evolve a variety of defence mechanisms to protect themselves. One obvious defence is the development of thorns or spines to slow down the feeding rate. These may grow all over the plant, from leaf to stem to trunk. Giraffe and Black Rhino (page 18), however, have thick, leathery tongues, and are mostly undeterred by thorns on new twigs and branches.

Some trees form relationships with ants, whereby the ants protect the trees from browsers, and in return receive sugars from the plant. Some Acacia thorn trees, being highly nutritious, produce both tannins and thorns.

▲ **Buffalo-thorn Jujube** ►
Ziziphus mucronata
Fruit: Jan - Aug
(3 - 10 m) 447

The Buffalo-thorn Jujube carries its thorns in pairs, one straight and one hooked. The zigzag branchlets and twigs, exceptionally shiny leaves and berry-like fruit are characteristic features. It is the burial tree of the Zulu and Sotho, and branches are laid on the graves of chiefs and royalty. Black Rhino and nyala browse the fruit and leaves.

◄ **African Migrant**
Catopsilia florella
(40 - 45 mm)

This butterfly is yellow in the wet season and white in the dry season. It migrates in vast numbers, and frequently congregates on flowers.

◄ ▲ **Sickle-bush** ►
Dichrostachys cinerea
(2 - 6 m) 190

Often forming dense thickets, these bushes encroach into open areas, but provide protection for many animals. They are recognised in summer by their flowers resembling Chinese lanterns, and in winter by their very nutritious, tightly coiled pods. Roots, bark, pods and leaves are used medicinally, including treatment of snakebites and toothache.

◄ Umbrella Acacia ►
Acacia tortilis
(3 - 6 m) 188

All **Acacias** have twice-compound feathery leaves, and hooked or straight thorns. While the **Umbrella Acacia** has tiny leaves, and both hooked and straight thorns, the **Scented-pod Acacia** has huge white, straight thorns. The Umbrella Acacia is also recognisable by its dense, umbrella-like crown and tightly curled pods. The pods of the Scented-pod Acacia look like a string of beads. All antelope enjoy the pods of both species.

▼ Scented-pod Acacia ►
Acacia nilotica
(5 - 10 m)179

▼ Processionary Moth and Worm ►
Anaphe reticulata
(Moth wingspan: 16 - 26 mm; worm: 5 cm)

The Processionary Moth is a silk moth. The larvae, known as Processionary Worms, live in gregarious colonies of up to about 600. The caterpillars can be seen either bunched tightly together on their food plant or moving through the bush, head to tail, in a long line.

▼ Greenthorn Torchwood ►
(Y-thorned Torchwood)
Balanites maughamii (8 - 20 m) 251

The Greenthorn Torchwood has some very unusual, distinctive features. It has a deeply multi-fluted trunk, forked green spines, and zigzag branchlets and twigs that grow outwards, giving it a thorny appearance. As it prefers a specific habitat, it is not common everywhere. The fruit, although eaten by humans and many animals, will kill snails, tadpoles and fish. Extract of the bark is used to induce vomiting.

olden Orbweb Spider ▼
lephilia senegalensis
25 - 30 mm)

his spider's golden orb-shaped eb, laden with dew, is a pectacular early morning sight. he webs are often threaded mong thorn trees. hey are very strong, nd capture large sects.

Trees

Open Areas

Flat open areas have soils that are mostly derived from the erosion of basalt or gabbro rocks (page v). These clay soils are usually high in nutrients. The trees that are easiest to identify are Knob-thorn Acacia and Marula trees that grow in dense stands (pages 2 - 3). Some other trees growing in these open areas are easy to spot because they bear seasonally striking fruit or flowers, such as the Monkey-orange and Purple-pod Cluster-leaf.

Brackish sites are flat, open patches found along rivers and drainage lines where salts accumulate in the soil. Trees and grasses growing here can tolerate these more salty soils, and are very palatable. Brackish areas can easily be identified by the presence of Magic Guarri bushes.

Purple Tip ►
Colotis ione
(45 - 50 mm)
(M)

These two **Colotis species** can be recognised by the stunning purple and orange tips to their wings. The **Purple Tip** is a fast-flying butterfly that dodges rapidly through open savannah. It is fond of rivers and dry river beds. The **Orange Tip** favours low-lying, hot areas, but avoids forests and slopes. It will fly throughout the year if conditions are right.

(M)

▲ Orange Tip
Colotis evenina evenina
(40 - 45 mm)

◄▲ Black Monkey-orange ▼
Strychnos madagascariensis
Fruit: Nov - Dec
(5 - 8 m) 626

Both these trees are **seasonally striking**. The **Purple-pod Cluster-leaf** has conspicuous purple pods for most of summer, autumn and winter. The hard, green seeds inside the pods are eaten by Brown-headed Parrots, baboon and monkey. The **Black Monkey-orange** carries orange-sized green fruit for most of the year, which turn bright yellow when ripe. A range of animals eat various parts of the tree. Humans eat the fruit pulp, but avoid the seeds, which act as a purgative.

◄ Purple-pod Cluster-leaf
(Lowveld Cluster-leaf)
Terminalia prunioides (3 - 7 m) 550

ushveld Gardenia ►
ardenia volkensii
3 - 10 m) 691

▲ Magic Guarri ▼
Euclea divinorum
(4 - 6 m) 595

In **brackish flats** the following three trees are common. Characteristics of **Bushveld Gardenia** are the pale-grey bark, large green woody fruit and attractive white flowers. The tree was believed to have magical powers used to keep evil spirits away. The **Magic Guarri** grows in groups, as dense, multi-stemmed bushes with shiny, wavy but leathery leaves. They are unpalatable, and seldom eaten by browsers. The frayed edges of twigs are very effective toothbrushes. The **Jacket-plum** has leathery berry-like fruit, which split open to reveal a bright red jelly covering black seeds. The fruit is eaten by a wide variety of mammals and birds, and humans use it to make jelly and vinegar.

▼ Jacket-plum ►
Pappea capensis
(up to 10 m)
433

(F)

◄ Brown-veined Migrant
Belenois aurota
Visible all year (40 - 45 mm)
Favouring open country, this butterfly migrates in late summer in large numbers (south-west to north-east).

Trees

Rivers and Drainage Lines

The trees that grow along the rivers are often the most striking, and by far the largest, Lowveld trees. Many have shallow root systems, to prevent the tree from drowning during high-rainfall periods. These trees, however, are vulnerable during droughts. If the underground water supplies dry up, their roots cannot reach water, and they will die.

The amount of water we use every day affects many other people, as well as the trees and animals that need water to survive. South Africa is a semi-arid country, and water is one of our most valuable resources.

◄ Ebony Jackal-berry ▼
Diospyros mespiliformis
(10 - 20 m) 606
The Ebony Jackal-berry has a massive gnarled or fluted trunk, and trunk-size branches. The leaves are conspicuously wavy, dark green above and paler below. Many animals and birds eat the green berries.

◄ Weeping Boer-bean ▼
Schotia brachypetala
(15 - 25 m) 202
The canopy of the Weeping Boer-bean curves downwards, and hanging branches may be bare from browsing. It has spectacular dark-crimson flowers in summer. The seeds of the bean-like pods are roasted for eating.

▼ Wild Date-pal
Phoenix reclinata (3 - 6 m)
This is the only indigenous Lowveld tree wi large, fern-like leaves and small, date-like fru Elephants eat many parts of the tree, wh humans eat the fruit, use the sap to brew be and weave mats and hats from the leaves. I found only on riverbanks and in riverbeds.

◄ Sycomore Fig ▼▲
Ficus sycomorus (5 - 25 m) 66
The massive yellow-pinkish trunk, with smooth bark, peeling in papery sections, makes this tree unmistakeable. The masses of clustered figs are produced all year round, and are eaten by numerous animals and birds. Green Pigeons (page 44), Brown-headed Parrots (page 42), hornbills, barbets and rollers relish the fruit.

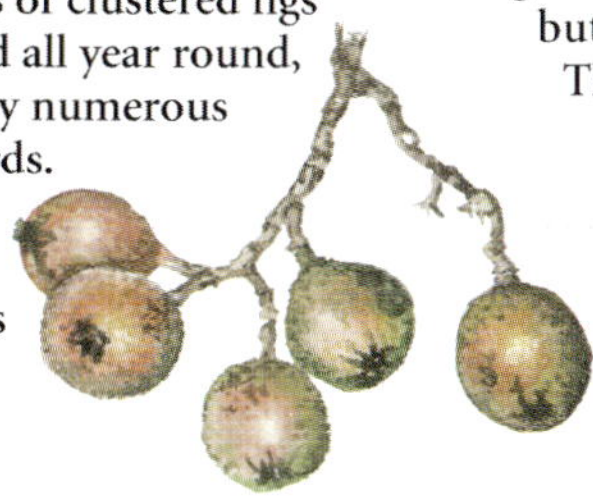

(M)

Lowveld Yellow ►
Eurema hecabe solifera
Visible all year
(35 - 40 mm)
This butterfly may be seen flying weakly in grass of the Lowveld, but it favours riverine vegetation. The caterpillars feed on Acacias.

◄ Sausage-tree ►
Kigelia africana
Flowers: Jul - Oct
(6 - 20 m) 678
The huge, sausage-like fruit is visible for most of the year and makes this tree unmistakeable. Not all trees carry fruit. Large, red flowers drop to form a red carpet on the ground. Numerous animals, birds and insects eat different parts of the tree.

(M)

Dancing Acraea
Acraea eponina manjaca
Visible Nov - June
(35 - 40 mm)
This very common butterfly may be seen flying in and out of tall grass at the edges of forests and woodlands.

◄ Tamboti ▼
Spirostachys africana
(5 - 10 m) 341
The rough, dark-brown to black bark, neatly cracked into regular rectangles, is the Tamboti's most striking feature. Broken branches produce a poisonous, extremely irritant, milky latex. Smoke from fires made from this wood can cause severe illness.

Flowers and Fruit

A wide variety of beautiful flowers grow here naturally, but only a few of the most common species are illustrated. Wild flowers have many uses for humans, from cooking to medicine and magic potions. Aesthetically, they surprise, delight and even awe us with their colours, shapes and smells. Bulbous plants store water and nutrients in their bulbs, and start flowering as temperatures rise in spring. Because they have green shoots when everything else is dry, they protect themselves against herbivores by producing bitter substances that often contain poisons. These can kill domestic stock, but not the game that has evolved alongside the plants.

Rivers, Drainage Lines and Marshes

The flowers on these two pages prefer wet areas. Four other plants that produce distinctive odours, which can be used to identify a particular species, are included as well.

Many exotic flowers have been introduced into South African gardens, but because they do not have any natural enemies, such as insects, they often replace the indigenous species in their natural environment. In the Lowveld two of the most invasive species are Prickly Pear and Lantana.

◄ **Jelly Melon**
Cucumis metuliferus
Dec - Jun (stems: up to 8 m)
Named after its cucumber-like, red fruit, this climber prefers shady places along drainage lines. Its leaves are cooked as spinach.

African Leopard ►
Phalanta phalantha aethiopica
Visible in summer (40 - 45 mm)
This common butterfly is a fast and restless flier, and when perching moves its wings constantly. It prefers wooded savannahs.

(M)

◄ **Plumbago**
Plumbago auriculata
Nov - Jan (up to 2 m)
Plumbago is a scrambling, shade-loving shrub that grows along drainage lines. The striking blue flowers attract butterflies. It is a popular garden plant.

◄ **Shaving-brush Bushwillow (Knobbly Creeper)**
Combretum mossambicense
Aug - Nov (creeper 545.1)

▲ **Flame Climbing Bushwillow (Flame Creeper)**
Combretum microphyllum
Aug - Nov (creeper 545)

These **scrambling, climbing shrubs** grow along rivers and both have pincushion flowers which are red (**Flame Creeper**) and white-to-pink (**Knobbly Creeper**). They are very conspicuous in early spring when their flowers stand out among the riverine vegetation. The Knobbly Creeper is found further away from rivers. The characteristic, four-winged pods typical of the Combretum family are visible on the Flame Creeper, but the Knobbly Creeper usually has five-winged pods (Nov to Jan).

◄ **Water Lily (Blue Lotus)**
Nymphaea nouchali caerulea
Aug - Mar
(flower diameter: up to 11 cm)
The Water Lily is rooted in the mud floor of ponds and quiet streams. The flower has a lovely scent, which attracts many insects. African Jacana (page 49) walk on the lily pads to move across a water surface. The tuber is eaten by hippos and monkeys, and is cooked as a vegetable by humans.

Flame Lily
Gloriosa superba
Nov - Mar (creeper)
This delicate creeper has striking red-and-yellow flowers. The bulb, deeply buried, is shaped like an ostrich foot. All parts of the plant contain a heart poison, and are very toxic. It grows along drainage lines.

River Lily ►
Crinum macowanii
Oct - Dec (up to 90 cm)
This lovely, rare, bulbous lily grows in waterlogged grasslands. It makes an attractive garden plant.

Jasmine ►
Jasminum fluminense
All year (up to 7 m)
Jasmine can be a woody, climbing shrub or sometimes a small tree. It occurs along rivers, scrambling over other plants.

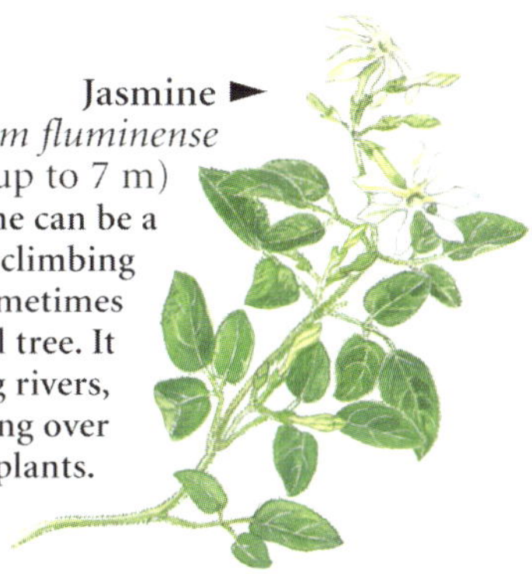

Potato Bush ▼
Phyllanthus reticulatus
Sep - Oct
(up to 8 m)
311

◄ **Wild Basil**
Ocimum gratissimum
Sep - Jun
(up to 2 m)

These four plants produce **characteristic odours. Wild Basil** and **Wild Aniseed** are perennial herbs or shrubs used medicinally and in cooking. Wild Basil is lemon- or clove-scented, with toothed leaf-margins and white flowers. Wild Aniseed has a liquorice scent, smooth leaf-margins and mauve-to-white flowers. The **Gifappel** is a vigorous climber, with triangular-shaped leaves (80 mm), which when crushed give off an unpleasant smell of rotting cabbage. However the leaves are cooked as spinach. The flowers are creamy-orange, and the round, yellow fruit is softly spiny with sticky, red seeds. The small, yellow flowers of the **Potato Bush** give off a potato-like odour, often noticed near rivers. It is particularly strong on spring and summer evenings in the Lowveld.

'ild Aniseed ►
cimum
nericanum
ll year
p to 80 cm)

Gifappel ►
Momordica foetida
Nov - Feb
(up to 7 m)

Flowers and Fruit

Disturbed Areas and Grasslands

After substantial rains a wide variety of flowers can be seen, especially in areas where the grass cover has been removed or disturbed. These flowering plants prepare the bare soil for grasses to re-establish themselves.

These pages illustrate the flowers found in disturbed areas (left-hand side) and in grassland (right-hand side).

◄ **Wing-seeded Sesame**
Sesamum alatum
Jan - Mar (up to 1 m)
This tall annual is common along the roadsides, and the dry stalks can still b seen during the dry months. It is also found in grasslands. The leaves and roots were formerly used to treat measles, and the seeds are edible.

Yellow Cleome ►
Cleome angustifolia
Dec - Mar
(up to 1,5 m)
This forb prefers sandy or rocky soil. It is often the most common flower in disturbed ground, and may cover large areas.

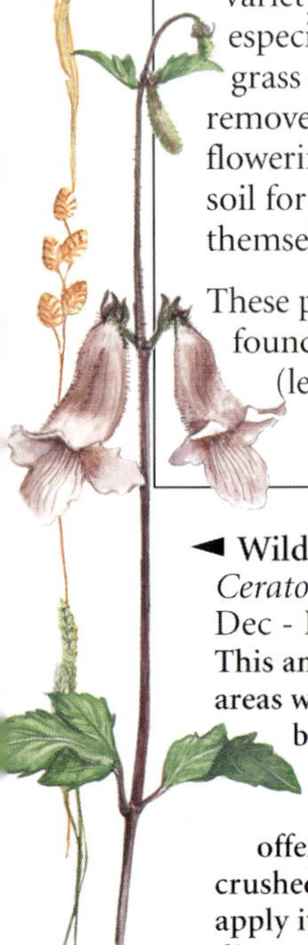

◄ **Wild Foxglove**
Ceratotheca triloba
Dec - Feb (up to 2 m)
This annual will grow in areas where the topsoil has been removed, particularly along roadsides. It has an offensive smell when crushed, and humans apply it to nails to discourage nail-biting.

◄ **Hammel Stertjie**
(String of Stars / Wild Heliotrope)
Heliotropium steudneri
Sep - Mar (up to 80 cm)
Masses of the white 'lamb's tail' flowers of this perennial herb may be seen along the roadside during summer. This plant contains an alkaloid that causes liver damage when eaten by animals in large quantities.

◄ **Violet**
Aptosimum lineare
Aug - Feb (5 - 12 cm)
This small herb grows close to the ground, especially in sandy patches and disturbed areas. It has long, lance-shaped leaves and deep-blue or purple flowers.

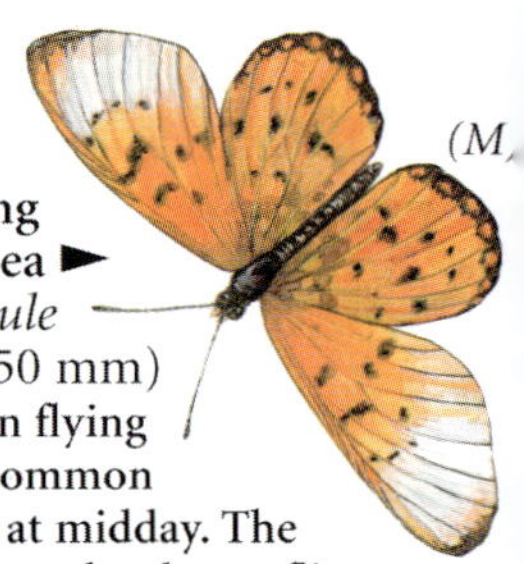

Wandering Donkey Acraea ►
Acraea neobule neobule
Visible all year (45 - 50 mm)
This common species can be seen flying singly all year round. It is a common sight around rocky outcrops at midday. The males can often be seen chasing other butterflies.

▼ **Yellow Pansy**
Junonia hierta cebrene
Visible all year (35 - 40 mm)
This attractive butterfly usually flies close to the ground, preferring open ground, grassy spots and gardens. Males can be spotted resting on their territories, usually flat bare ground, with their wings open.

Wild Morning Glory (Leafy-flowered Ipomoea) ▼
Ipomoea crassipes
Sep - Jan (stems: up to 1 m)
An erect or trailing perennial, often seen hanging from other vegetation or in short grassland in disturbed areas. The roots are eaten raw by humans, and are used as a love potion and to ensure prosperity.

◄ Impala Lily
Adenium multiflorum
May - Sep (up to 2 m)
The striking flowers of this succulent shrub are visible in open areas and rocky outcrops. The large, cigar-shaped pods burst open when ripe to release masses of small seeds tufted with long white hairs. All parts contain a poisonous milky latex that has been used as a fish poison and on arrow tips.

Tumbleweed (Ground Lily) ►
Ammocharis coranica
Oct - Dec (up to 20 cm)
Tumbleweed is a perennial bulb that grows in clumps in open, often brackish patches near pans. The flowers are silvery pink, sweetly scented, and beautiful when they bloom together after rain.

Vernonia ►
Vernonia fastigiata
Oct - May (up to 1 m)
A bushy, annual herb, its leaves have been used to flavour food.

Eastern Rhigozum (Mopaniegranaat) ▼
Rhigozum zambesiacum
Sep - Dec (up to 7 m)
This spiny shrub is very conspicuous when covered in yellow flowers after the first rains. It is most common in brackish sites and in open areas (page xiv), and on rocky hillsides (page xvi).

◄ Plakkie
Cotyledon orbiculata
Mar - Sep (up to 1,5 m)
An evergreen shrub, this Cotyledon may be identified by its succulent, round, grey-green leaves with deep-reddish margins. It prefers to grow on rocky outcrops on grassy slopes. The Afrikaans name 'Plakkie' is derived from its use as a poultice (a heated leaf) on boils or abscesses.

Wandering Jew ► (Blue Commelina)
Commelina erecta
Nov - Feb (20 - 50 cm)
A low-growing, perennial herb with upright or spreading stems. The leaves are narrow, and fold upwards.

Wild Hibiscus ►
Hibiscus engleri
Dec - May (up to 1 m)
This shrublet is easy to recognise by its yellow flower with a striking dark-reddish centre. The stems carry sharply pointed star-shaped bristles.

MAMMALS

There is an amazing diversity and abundance of mammal life in the Lowveld. However, only a certain amount of food and habitat space are available. The animals are able to live together and share resources by occupying different niches. Niche separation relates to time, (some animals are active during the day, others at night); or to space, (some animals live in open areas, others in a dense habitat). Cheetah avoid lion and leopard by hunting in open areas during daylight hours. Leopard drag their prey up trees to prevent it being stolen by other carnivores.

The animals have also evolved certain behavioural strategies to help them survive. The herbivorous (plant-eating) mammals may be browsers, or grazers, or both. Browsers usually live in smaller groups in bushy or wooded areas. They either stand completely still or scatter when threatened, using the vegetation as camouflage or cover from predators. Grazers often live on open grassy plains in large groups because many individuals together have a better chance of detecting predators.

Mammals are measured in height H – ground to shoulder, or in length L – tip of nose to tip of tail.

Dominance is the difference between life and death in adult male lions. Here sub-adults build skills through play (see also page 21).

Animals You Cannot Miss

These huge animals consume so much food that they act as modifiers of the landscape. Elephant thin out densely wooded areas, making habitats more suitable for animals such as wildebeest and zebra. White Rhino create their own 'grazing lawns', which may suit animals like impala but not bushbuck. A large herd of buffalo can even trample down tall grassland, so that the visibility improves. The grassland then becomes suitable for zebra which previously avoided the area. Hippo change the riverine habitat by eating the surrounding grasses. They also transfer nutrients from adjacent land back into the river, to feed fish and invertebrates. Giraffe have less impact, but are frequently seen, and are fascinating to watch.

These animals form an important part of an ecosystem, changing the environment enough to make an area more, or less, suitable for a wide variety of species.

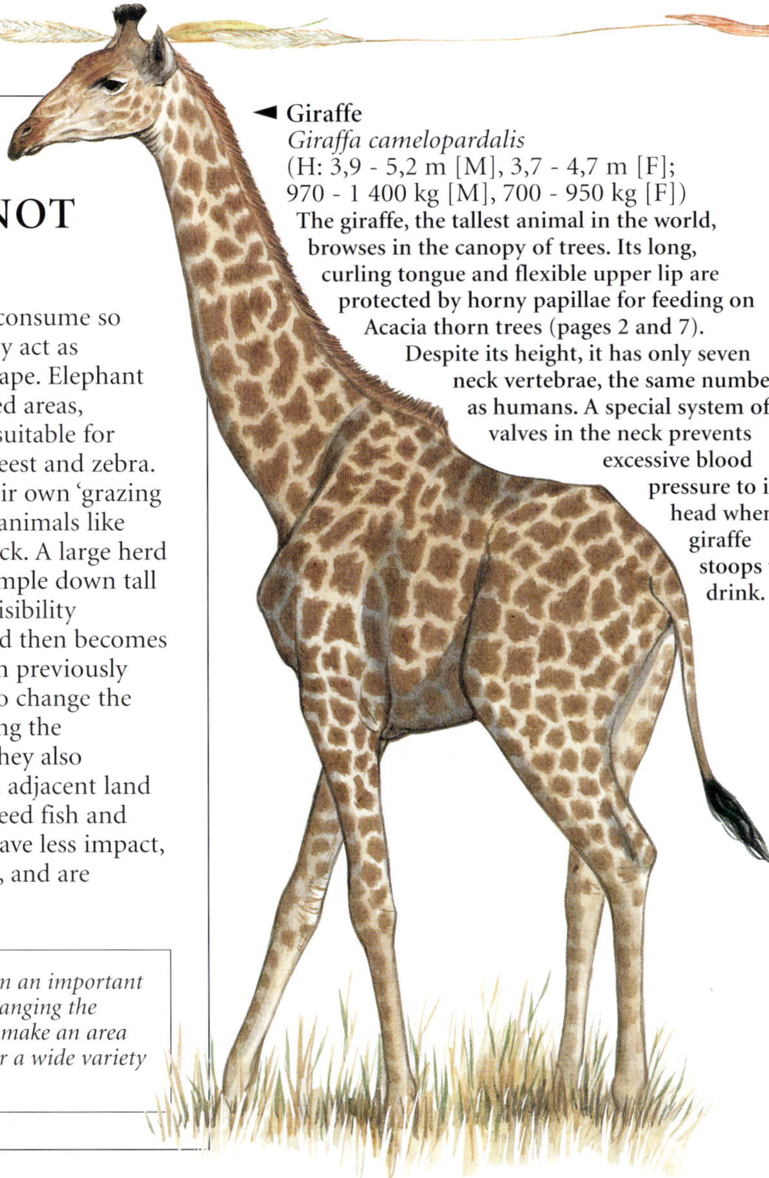

◄ **Giraffe**
Giraffa camelopardalis
(H: 3,9 - 5,2 m [M], 3,7 - 4,7 m [F]; 970 - 1 400 kg [M], 700 - 950 kg [F])

The giraffe, the tallest animal in the world, browses in the canopy of trees. Its long, curling tongue and flexible upper lip are protected by horny papillae for feeding on Acacia thorn trees (pages 2 and 7). Despite its height, it has only seven neck vertebrae, the same number as humans. A special system of valves in the neck prevents excessive blood pressure to its head when th giraffe stoops to drink.

Visitors often comment that **rhinos** look prehistoric! The **Black Rhino** has a hook-lip, which it uses for browsing, while the **White Rhino** has a square lip, adapted for grazing. As a result, the White Rhino is found in open savannah, and the Black Rhino in dense bush or thickets. The calf of the White Rhino walks in front of the mother, while the Black Rhino calf follows behind. The Black Rhino is slightly smaller, and far more aggressive.

◄ Black Rhinoceros
Diceros bicornis
(H: 1,6 - 2,0 m; 800 - 1 100 kg; record horn 1,05 m)

White Rhinoceros ►
Ceratotherium simum
(H: 1,8 m; 1 600 - 2 300 kg; record horn 1,58 m)

◄ Hippopotamus
Hippopotamus amphibius
(H: 1,5 m; 1 500 kg; tusk-like canines 10 - 30 cm)

▲ Buffalo
Syncerus caffer
(H: 1,6 m; 750 kg; record horn 1,29 m)

These **large, bulk grazers** have totally different lifestyles. **Hippos** spend all day in the water, but at night may cover many kilometers feeding on short grass. They are gregarious, living in pods of about 15, with dominant bulls. It is very dangerous to be between a hippo and the water. Their huge bulk may appear slow, but they are exceptionally fast on land. **Buffalo** prefer the open savannah with tall, coarse grass for feeding. They live in herds of up to 500, although old, solitary bulls are often seen. A buffalo will raise its nose into the air to try to catch the scent of a predator. Old, hot-tempered bulls can charge unexpectedly, and the buffalo is therefore considered one of Africa's most dangerous species.

Elephant ►
Loxodonta africana
(H: 3,2 - 4,0 m [M], 2,5 - 3,4 m [F]; 5 000 - 6 300 kg [M], 2 800 - 3 500 kg [F]; record tusk 102,3 kg)

Elephants live in stable social units led by a matriarch. Mature bulls form bachelor groups, or are seen wandering alone. The elephant uses its highly dexterous trunk in every aspect of its life, from drinking and feeding to communication. It flaps its large ears, rich in blood vessels, to get rid of excess heat. Elephants are generally peaceful animals, but can become extremely aggressive if harassed, threatened or sick.

▼ Koppie Charaxes
Charaxes jasius saturnus
Insect (75 - 100 mm)

Charaxes species are often seen sucking fluid from elephant dung, or the sap of damaged trees. Males of the Koppie Charaxes often visit the tops of ridges and koppies at midday. The caterpillar's food includes Boer-bean species (page 10).

(F)

Large Carnivores

These large hunters have always fascinated humans, perhaps because we are basically hunters too. Carnivores are at the top of the food chain, preying on herbivores. They are well adapted for hunting, with excellent eyesight and hearing, sharp teeth, and bodies designed for speed and/or power. Scavengers have an acute sense of smell to help them locate dead carcasses. Their teeth and jaws are exceptionally powerful for grinding bones.

All predators are opportunistic, seizing the easiest chances to catch prey. They eliminate the old, sick and weak animals first, while the strongest and fittest survive. Predators therefore play an important role in the ecosystem, helping to maintain strong, healthy herbivore populations.

Humans are not perceived as being natural prey. However, a sudden movement, standing up, or a loud noise can create a potentially dangerous situation in an open landrover.

◄ Wild Dog
Lycaon pictus
(H: 68 cm; 24 - 30 kg)

The Wild Dog is diurnal, and is an endangered species. Wild Dogs are highly co-operative, hunting and breeding in packs of up to 40 animals. Wild Dogs don't conceal themselves when hunting. They chase their prey for several kilometres to the point of exhaustion. One dog may grab the prey by the muzzle, allowing the other dogs to disembowel it. The pack is headed by one breeding pair, but the other members help to look after and feed the young.

◄ Black-backed Jacka
Canis mesomelas
(H: 38 cm; 6 - 10 k

◄ Side-striped Jackal
Canis adustus
(H: 40 cm; 8 - 10 kg)

These two species of **jackal** are not really direct competitors. The **Black-backed Jackal** favours more open savannah grassland. The **Side-striped Jackal** prefers thickly wooded country. The Side-striped Jackal is more strictly nocturnal, and less often seen. Jackals are efficient hunters, killing whatever is available – young antelope, rodents, hares, birds, reptiles, fish and insects, and both species will scavenge readily, following predators. They also eat fruit and berries (Ebony Jackal-berry page 10). Pairs mate for life.

◄ **Spotted Hyaena** ►
Crocuta crocuta
(H: 70 - 80 cm; 65 - 70 kg)

Hyaena are social, living in clans of 4 - 18 animals, headed by a large matriarch. They are predominantly nocturnal, but are also active during the day. Although renowned scavengers, they are also highly effective predators. Their distinctive '*whoooo-oop*' call can be heard across the Lowveld at night.

Cheetah ►
Acinonyx jubatus
(H: 80 cm; 40 - 60 kg)

◄ **Leopard**
Panthera pardus
(H: 70 - 80 cm;
40 - 70 kg)

These three large **carnivores** have different lifestyles. The **leopard** is a solitary and secretive animal. It spends most of its day in hiding. It hunts by ambushing its prey, and lives in dense bush, forest or rocky areas. **Cheetah** need open areas to hunt, as they rely on speed to catch their prey. They are the fastest land mammals on Earth, with estimated top speeds of about 100 km/h. Although solitary, some males form small coalitions, and females are often seen with their young. **Lions** (photo page 16) are social animals that observe a strict hierarchy within the pride. Although lionesses do most of the hunting, males that are present feed first, followed by females and cubs. When food is scarce, cubs cannot compete with adults, and 80% of cubs born may starve to death. Lions require some concealment for stalking, then cover the final distance in a fast charge.

A type of carnivore hierarchy exists in the savannah, depending on the size and strength of the animal and its group. Lions are usually the dominant predator, and may inflict serious losses on Wild Dog and cheetah populations sharing the same habitat.

◄ **Lion** ►
Panthera leo
(H: 1 m;
180 - 230 kg [M],
113 - 160 kg [F])

Grazers

Animals that prefer open areas are usually grazers, and they tend to congregate in large groups. Visibility is very important, as their best defence is to spot predators early enough to be able to escape. The main predators here are lion and cheetah. Grazers share available grasses by using different parts of the grass layer, or choosing different types of grass. Some species feed selectively, such as Common Reedbuck, while others, such as zebra, feed on a wide range of grasses. This means that there is more food to go around, and less competition.

Some herbivores establish beneficial relationships with one another, such as zebra and wildebeest. Their feeding habits are complementary, and because they graze together there are more eyes and ears to warn against stalking predators.

The interactions between plants, animals and the environment are interdependent. Each part plays an invaluable role in the survival of the whole system.

▼ **Warthog**
Phacochoerus aethiopicus (H: 70 cm; 60 - 100 kg; tusks 12 cm [M], 3 cm [F])
Warthogs, named for their facial warts, live in family groups. They have poor eyesight, and may approach quite close to visitors, rooting about on their knees. When disturbed, they spend a few seconds staring, then run off with tails held erect. They shelter at night in old aardvark holes (page 59).

▼ **Dung Beetle**
Family *Scarabaeidae*
Insect (5 - 50 mm)
Dung Beetles are often seen rolling fresh dung into balls. An egg is laid inside the ball, which the beetle may bury underground. They clean up decaying matter and carry nutrients underground, playing an important role in the ecosystem.

(M)

◄ **Waterbuck** ►
Kobus ellipsiprymnus
(H: 1,7 m [M], 1,3 m [F]; 260 kg [M], 230 kg [F]; horn 75 cm)
Lyre-shaped, forward-pointing horns, and the white ring around the rump, make the waterbuck unmistakeable. When pursued, it often takes refuge in water, and swims readily. Waterbuck live in small herds, in tall-to-medium grass and hilly areas close to water.

(M)

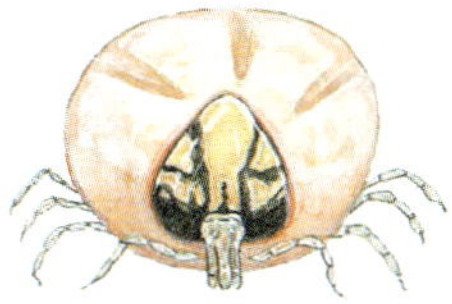

(F)

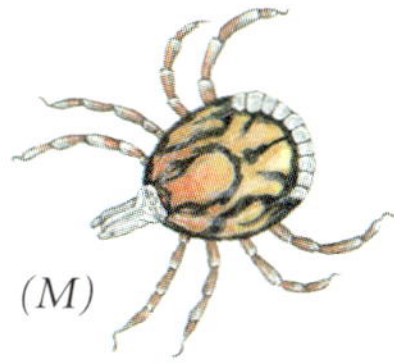

(M)

Heart-water Tick (Bontbosluis) ▲►
Amblyoma hebreaum
Insect relative (3 - 12 mm)
The tick larvae are called pepper ticks because of their minute size. When the eggs hatch on the ground, the larvae of many species crawl up and hang in clusters (2 000 - 20 000) at the ends of vegetation, waiting for a host to pass by. All ticks transmit human and animal diseases, such as tick bite fever. This tick transmits heart-water in cattle, but wild animals are not susceptible. In tick-infested areas, visitors should examine themselves regularly, and remove any ticks found on the skin.

Larvae (pepper-grain size)

Common Reedbuck ►
Redunca arundinum
(H: 90 cm; horn 30 cm)
Common Reedbuck prefer tall grass near water, and will swim when in extreme danger. They have a sharp alarm whistle, and flee in a rocking-horse motion with their tails fanned over their backs. Calves are hidden to protect them from predation.

◄ **Plains Zebra (Burchell's Zebra)**
Equus burchelli antiquorum
(H: 1,3 m; 290 - 340 kg)

Blue Wildebeest ►
Connochaetes taurinus
(H: 1,5 m [M], 1,35 m [F]; 250 kg [M], 180 kg [F]; horn 60 cm)

Zebra and Blue Wildebeest are both **highly gregarious herd animals**, breeding in spring and summer. They often graze together. **Zebra** feed on taller grass, and are often in the presence of **wildebeest**, which prefer short grass. Both wildebeest and zebra rely on each other's eyesight and alertness. In addition, the zebra's stripes confuse predators: when the herd bunches together it appears to be a single unit.

Browsers

The savannah areas, which are covered with trees, provide shelter and food for many species, especially browsers. Many browsers have narrow muzzles to pick the fine, nutritious leaves off Acacia thorn-trees (pages 2 and 7). Browsers have adapted to the defence mechanisms of trees that are designed to reduce excessive browsing. By moving from tree to tree they avoid eating large amounts of deterrent chemicals (page 4).

Like grazers, browsers eat different parts of the vegetation, which means that there is more food available to a variety of animals. Giraffe feed in the top parts of the canopy, kudu in the middle, while smaller antelope, like steenbok, feed only on small bushes or trees. Elephant eat at every level, and often include bark, pods and fruit in their diet.

The different types of vegetation on the crests and valleys (page x) provide animals with the opportunity to choose the most palatable diet. The fresh, green grass on the crest gives the grasses in the valleys a chance to recover from winter grazing.

(M)

▲ **Impala**
Apyceros melampus
(H: 90 cm; 45 kg; horn 50 cm)
Impala are usually the most common antelope, browsing and grazing in variable size herds of up to 100. When alarmed they 'blow' or 'snort'. While running they confuse predators with enormous leaps of up to 3 metres high and 11 metres long. At mating time, around April and May, the snorting and grunting of rutting males can be heard over great distances.

(F) *(M)*

▲ **Steenbok**
Raphicerus campestris
(H: 50 cm; 11 kg; horn 9 cm)

◄ **Klipspringer**
Oreotragus oreotragus
(H: 60 cm;
11 kg [M],
13 kg [F];
horn 8 cm)

It is not difficult to distinguish between these three **small browsers**. The **steenbok** live in the plains or open savannah. **Klipspringer** are very territorial, and inhabit rocky hills or koppies. Both these species obtain most of their water from juicy plants, and are therefore unusual in not being dependent on water. The **Common Duiker** is found in the undergrowth and thickets along watercourses, browsing leaves, fruit, flowers and seeds. Both the duiker and the steenbok are mostly solitary, except when breeding. Klipspringer live in pairs or small family groups.

◄ **Kudu**
Tragelaphus strepsiceros
(H: 1,4 - 1,5 m; 250 kg [M], 180 kg [F]; horn 1,2 m)

▼ **Bushbuck**
Tragelaphus scriptus
(H: 70 - 80 cm; 45 kg [M], 30 kg [F]; horn 26 cm)

These three antelope are **large browsers**. They live in small groups, and may appear similar. **Kudu,** however, frequent dense savannah and hilly terrain, while **nyala** move around riverine bush. Kudu males have long spiralled horns, and although the horns of nyala males also twist, they are shorter. Kudu are extremely agile, and can jump 2-metre-high fences from a standing position. Both species bark when alarmed.

Bushbuck are smaller than nyala, and the males' horns are straighter. They have stripes along the sides like kudu and nyala, but may be recognised by the white spots on their flanks. They are often seen alone, near rivers, but are shy and secretive and move about in the thickets and dense undergrowth.

▼ **Common Duiker**
Sylvicapra grimmia
(H: 50 cm; 18 kg [M], 21 kg [F]; horn 11 cm)

▲ **Nyala**
Tragelaphus angasii
(H: 1,1 m [M], 1 m [F]; 110 kg [M], 60 kg [F]; horn 60 cm)

Other Interesting Mammals

There are other interesting mammals in the Lowveld that are not part of the larger carnivore and herbivore groups. They are mostly omnivorous, feeding on both plant and animal life. They too fill a specific niche within the environment, and have particular behavioural strategies best suited for survival.

One of the most interesting aspects of these creatures is the co-operation between species. Dwarf Mongooses often live in active termite mounds, where they favour the cooler temperatures found inside. They sometimes hunt with hornbills, which catch any insects the mongoose might disturb. In return the hornbills may warn them if any danger is approaching, such as an eagle.

Many of the smaller species cannot afford to be particular about their food choice, especially when resources are limited. These less specialised species often have a wide distribution, and survive better during hard times because of this adaptability.

▲**Vervet Monkey**
Cercopithecus aethiops
(L: 1 m; 5 kg)

▲**Banded Mongoose**
Mungos mungo
(L: 60 cm, 1,4 kg)

Slender Mongoose ►
Galerella sanguinea
(L: 58 cm; 710 g [M], 570 g [F])

Mongooses are all insectivorous. The **Banded Mongoose** lives in dense savannah in thickets and on rocky outcrops. The **Slender Mongoose** is solitary, often seen along the roadside, hunting rodents, reptiles, birds and insects. The **Dwarf Mongoose** prefers open savannah with termitaria or other hiding places. Both the Dwarf and Banded Mongoose are highly social, living in large groups of up to 30 animals. Birds of prey (pages 52 - 53) are the main enemies of mongooses.

oth these **primates** are social and omnivorous, ıt live in different habitats and behave ifferently. **Vervet Monkeys** are more common ıan **baboons**, and spend their time in the ees near rivers, using them for food, shelter ıd refuge. Baboons are ground-based, ınging across a variety of habitats. They eed rocky hills or habitats with tall trees ır sleeping, finding refuge and posting ıntries. The leopard (pages 21 and 78) their main predator.

Chacma Baboon ►
Papio ursinus
(L:1,35 m;
30 kg [M], 16 kg [F])

▼ Tree Squirrel
Paraxerus cepapi (L: 34 cm; 190 g)
Tree Squirrels live in small family groups, but forage on their own for fruit seeds, shoots, roots and insects. They are highly vocal, communicating with each other using a variety of calls. Group members share a nest and carry the same smell. Strangers lacking the family smell are chased off.

Honey Badger ►
Mellivora capensis (L: 95 cm; 12 kg)
Generally solitary, the Honey Badger feeds on rodents, reptiles, insects, larvae of Dung Beetles (page 22), eggs, ground birds, wild fruits and honey. It is exceptionally strong, and uses its long, sharp claws to dig for prey or to make a hole for sleeping and breeding. Honey Badgers are formidable fighters and predators, protecting themselves with courage and ferocity.

◄ Dwarf Mongoose
Helogale parvula (L: 38 cm, 260 g)

Reptiles, Amphibians and Fish

These creatures are often overlooked in the search for the large and impressive mammals. However, reptiles, amphibians and fish have their own exciting equivalents of meat-eaters, grazers and browsers. Watching a lion kill large prey like a buffalo is thrilling, but a python catching a dove or antelope could be just as interesting, and is much more unusual to see.

Only a very few of the common and more obvious creatures are covered on these pages. They are intended merely as an introduction to a new and different world.

Reptiles and amphibians are not always considered the most likeable creatures, but their curious habits and adaptations to the environments they occupy, tell a fascinating story.

Reptiles, amphibians and fish are measured in length from tip of nose to tip of tail.

In a life and death struggle the Grey Tree Frog (page 33) has lost out to a super reptilian predator, the Spotted Bush Snake.

Landbased

There is a greater diversity of reptiles than of mammals in southern Africa. They successfully inhabit most environments – land and water. Landbased reptiles have dry, scaly skin to protect them from the elements. They are all cold-blooded, needing the sun to keep them warm, but they differ enormously in appearance, habits and habitat.

Some species are strongly associated with specific trees, such as the Blue-headed Tree Agama with Acacias. Tortoises and lizards use termitaria for breeding and often for hunting, while hollow tree trunks are favourite shelters for a wide variety of lizards, monitors and even the Southern African Python.

Monitors and pythons have been endangered by the fashion industry because of their attractive skins, but are now protected species. Monitors are most often sighted when disturbed, as they scuffle rapidly across the ground, vanishing to safety.

◄ Leopard Tortoise
Geochelone pardalis
(30 - 60 cm)

These two **tortoises** are widely distributed in South Africa. They are most active during or just after the rains, and hibernate during cold winter months. The **Leopard Tortoise** and the **Bell's Hinged Tortoise** eat plants and fruit, but the latter also preys on millipedes, beetles and snails. The hatchlings of both species are vulnerable to predation by carnivorous animals and birds. Hinged Tortoises are named after the unique hing found at the back of the shell (of adults), which can be closed for protection.

Bell's Hinged Tortoise ▼
Kinixys belliana
(17 - 22 cm)

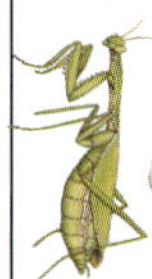

◄ Praying Mantis
Sphodromantis gastrica Insect (8 cm
A slow-moving, predatory insect, it sits back on its hind legs holding it front legs out together as if praying As soon as an insect passes by, the front legs shoot out and seiz the prey. It is included here as is a favourite prey of chameleons (below).

Flap-neck Chameleon ▼
Chamaeleo dilepis
(20 - 24 cm)

(Breeding M)

▲ Blue-headed Tree Agama
Acanthocerus atricollis
(20 - 30 cm)

These **lizard-like creatures** live above the ground. The **Tree Agama** gives a painful bite if teased by humans. It is often sighted on a tree trunk, where the blue head of a breeding male is unmistakeable. It may move to the ground to eat ants and termites. The **House Gecko** lives under tree bark, but may be seen actively hunting insects on the walls and roofs of homes at night. The males vigorously defend their territories, chasing or fighting off other males. A **Flap-neck Chameleon** can change colour to match its surroundings, thus escaping predators. It detects insects with its independently rotating eyes, and catches them with its 20-cm-long, sticky tongue. Rich folklore causes it to be feared by many tribes.

◄ Moreau's Tropical House Gecko
Hemidactylus mabouia (12- 16 cm)

Southern African Python ►
Python natalensis (3 - 5 m)
The non-venomous python usually hunts at night, detecting warm-blooded prey with the heat sensors on its lips. Birds, reptiles, small mammals, large antelope and monkeys are killed by suffocation, and swallowed. The female lays eggs in disused aardvark burrows (page 59). She protects them until they hatch.

◄ Puff Adder
Bitis arietans
(70 - 90 cm)

A bite from one of these **highly venomous** snakes can result in a human death. The **Puff Adder** has a flattened, triangular head and moves with a sluggish, caterpillar-like motion. It lies in cover, waiting to ambush its prey. It will warn an intruder of its presence by uttering a deep hiss. The **Boomslang** is recognised by its blunt head and very large eyes. The colouration is variable: juveniles are twig-coloured, females are olive to brown, and males have various colour phases (one being illustrated here). It inflates its throat and will bite readily if threatened. It hunts prey during the day, and when it has caught the prey, will chew it, to inject the venom.

(M)

▲ Boomslang
Dispholidus typus
(1,2 - 1,5 m)

Rock Monitor ►
Varanus exanthematicus albigularis (0,7 - 1,3 m)
This huge lizard eats tortoises, eggs, beetles, millipedes, small birds, rodents and carrion. It digs tunnels under rock overhangs, or uses old burrows or ermite mounds to shelter and hibernate in winter. Its eggs, which are often eaten by the Banded Mongoose (page 26), are laid in soft, moist soil.

◄ Giant Plated Lizard
Gerrhosaurus validus (40 - 60 cm)
These lizards are omnivorous, eating plant material, insects, snails, millipedes and other lizards. They inhabit the upper area of large granite outcrops or koppies. They use the rocks for shelter, protection and breeding.

Waterbased

Some reptiles have adapted to life in water. They feed on the aquatic life, and use the water to escape when threatened. Crocodiles, one of Africa's best known reptiles, lie in the rapids with their mouths open to catch fish moving down the river. Amphibians, although not always dependent on standing bodies of water, need moist habitats. Their slimy, porous skin, which is used for breathing, would otherwise dry out. Water is also needed for breeding. Frogs therefore thrive best in good rainy years. The foamy, white nests of the Grey Tree Frog (photo page 28) can be seen at most temporal pools.

There are as many diverse habitats under the water as there are above it. Fish habits and lifestyles are richly varied, and all fill a specific niche within the aquatic environment. Fish may have as elaborate breeding habits, and be as territorial and social, as birds and mammals. Their lives are not well understood, but they form another valuable link within the ecosystem.

Shortly after the first pools and pans have filled in summer, the loud mating calls of a wide variety of frogs pierce the night. Often the high-pitched musical calls or trills can be heard more than a kilometre away. These interesting creatures are very sensitive, and can only survive and breed in clean, uncontaminated pools.

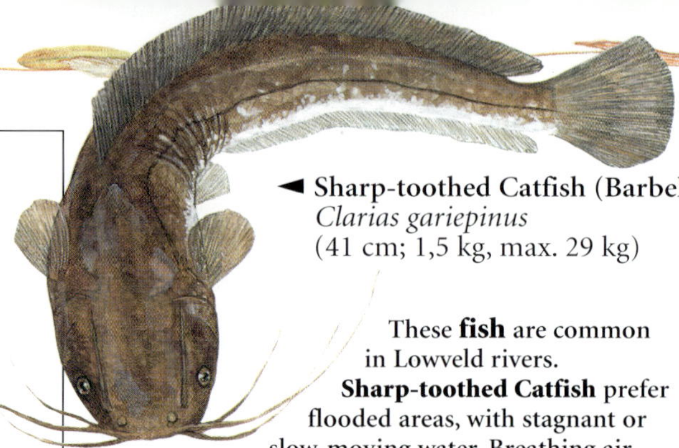

◄ Sharp-toothed Catfish (Barbel)
Clarias gariepinus
(41 cm; 1,5 kg, max. 29 kg)

These **fish** are common in Lowveld rivers. **Sharp-toothed Catfish** prefer flooded areas, with stagnant or slow-moving water. Breathing air, and walking on their front fins, they can move from one body of water to another, thus surviving drought. They are eaten by many animals, including Fish Eagles (page 50), crocodiles, leopards (page 21) and humans. **Tilapia** inhabit slow-moving rivers. The male constructs a saucer-shaped nest in the sand for the female to lay her eggs. She then sucks them into her mouth where she protects them until they hatch. The nests are often visible from the water surface, or if the pool dries up.

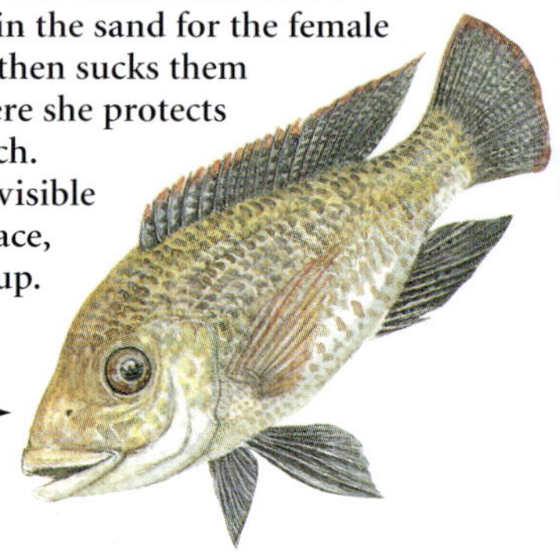

Mozambique Tilapia ►
Oreochromis mossambicus
(30 cm; 0,7 kg)

▼ Crocodile
Crocodylus niloticus (2,5 - 3,5 m)
The crocodile cannot function well at body temperatures below 25°C. It therefore basks in the sun during winter. Adults eat mostly fish, but also terrapins, birds and mammals. The female lays 50 - 70 eggs in a hole in the sand. When the young hatch, she carries them in her mouth to water, where they become independent immediately.

◄ Grey Tree Frog
(Foam-nest Frog)
Chiromantis xerampelina
(7 - 8 cm)

The female Grey Tree Frog secretes a fluid that is beaten to a foam by her back legs. The eggs are laid in the foam, which protects them from drying out and from predators. Most rainpools have foam nests on branches or rocks overhanging the water. Tadpoles spend a few days here before dropping into the water.

Bushveld Rain Frog ►
(Blaasop)
Breviceps adspersus
(7 cm)

These two **frogs walk and waddle**, rather than jump, and dig holes backwards for hibernation. **Rain Frogs** cannot swim, and appear for three months after the first rains to mate. Jelly-encapsulated eggs are laid in holes in the ground. The **Rubber Frog** lays about 600 eggs in a mass of soft jelly, attached to surface vegetation of pans and swamps.

◄ Red-banded Rubber Frog (Gomlastiekpadda)
Phrynomantis bifasciatus
(5 cm)

Mottled Olive Toad ►
Bufo garmani (3 - 10 cm)

These toads are large, covered with knobbly, rounded warts, and are common in open bushy country in damp places. They hunt insects, especially termites and moths, and are often seen on the road at night.

Water Monitor ►
Varanus niloticus
(1 - 1,4 m, max. 2 m)

The largest African lizard, the Water Monitor, eats crabs, mussels, fish, frogs and birds. During the day it basks in the sun on rocks and tree trunks near water. When threatened, it dives under water and swims to safety. Crocodiles and pythons prey on the adults.

▼ Serrated Hinged Terrapin
Pelusios sinuatus (30 - 40 cm)

Sometimes these terrapins are seen basking on rocks and logs during the day, or the tips of their noses are seen poking out of muddy waterholes and pans. They eat carrion, mussels, invertebrates and frogs, as well as the ticks off the immersed legs of buffalo standing in water to drink.

BIRDLIFE

An interest in birds ensures that a trip into the Lowveld will always be rewarding. Birds use a wide variety of habitats and food niches. The bills or beaks of birds tell a lot about their diet, and therefore about the food niche they occupy. Seed-eaters have small conical bills, and forage close to or on the ground; nectar-feeders have long thin bills, and feed on flowering trees or plants; many insect-eaters have hooked bills, and perch on a branch, waiting for prey to move within striking distance.

The larger predatory birds often perch high in tall trees, from where they scan the ground for prey. Otherwise they are sighted soaring and gliding above, looking for prey. Many of them breed in winter, when they are very active and easy to spot. In most of these raptor species the females are larger than the males, and tend to catch larger prey.

Birds are numbered with a Roberts number; their sizes are given from beak-tip to tail-tip.

African Jacanas occupy a very specific niche, walking on their long toes, on lily-pads, in quiet corners of relatively permanent water (see page 49).

Drier Bush away from Water

This habitat is fairly dry, and has a greater number of species during summer. It includes the denser bush away from water, as well as the more open areas with fewer trees, such as the brackish sites (page xiv). Different birds are found in different niches in drier bush. These have been divided into On or Near the Ground, Using Prominent Perches and In the Canopy of Trees.

On or Near the Ground

These birds spend a lot of time looking for food on the ground. When flushed or threatened they may settle in bushes and trees. Many of them are conspicuous, and are easily spotted foraging. Their characteristic calls can be heard ringing through the savannah.

Some bird calls are distinctive, attractive and easy to learn. These can help with bird identification, and will give you a new level of pleasure and awareness.

◄ **Crested Barbet**
Trachyphonus vaillantii
(23 cm) 473
This barbet is unmistakeable with its thick bill and colourful plumage. It is highly vocal, the call sounding like a bell-less alarm clock. The bill is used to dig nesting holes in tree trunks, where a pair raise up to four broods a season.

African Hoopoe ►
Upupa africana
(27 cm) 451
The African Hoopoe eats mainly caterpillars and worms, which it finds in the ground by probing with its long beak. It often erects its fan-shaped crest after landing, and flies as if its wings can't support its body weight. It says its name when calling '*hoop-hoop*'.

◄ **Emerald-spotted Wood-Dove**
Turtur chalcospilos (20 cm) 358
Usually solitary or in pairs, the Emerald-spotted Wood-Dove is most often seen on sandy roads or on bare ground where it eats seeds, berries and termites. It has an unmistakeable, melancholic call: *'Oh dear, dear, dear, dear'*.

Senegal Lapwing ►
(Lesser Black-winged Plover)
Vanellus lugubris (24 cm) 256
This migrant lapwing, with yellow-orange eyes and brown legs, is essentially a Mozambican bird, but can sometimes be seen here at the western point of its range. It favours dry savannahs, and especially burnt or heavily grazed areas. It is nomadic, occurring in small parties.

Crowned Lapwing ►
(Crowned Plover)
Vanellus coronatus
(30 cm) 255
Gregarious Crowned Lapwings, with their obvious crowns, are found in sparsely covered and burnt areas. They are renowned for their habit of dive-bombing intruders near their nests, with noisy screams.

◄ Arrow-marked Babbler
Turdoides jardineii
(24 cm) 560
Babblers move through the lower branches, from tree to tree, in a loose, noisy, babbling group of about ten birds. The group helps to build the nest in dense bush or trees, where only the dominant female breeds.

Red-billed Buffalo-Weaver ►
Bubalornis niger
(21 cm) 798
The nest of this weaver is large and conspicuous, an untidy mass of thorny twigs and sticks high up in the branches of a tree. The weavers breed communally, and each pair has its own entrance and tunnel into a nest.

(M)

Southern Ground-Hornbill ►
Bucorvus leadbeateri
(1,1 m) 463

Red-crested Korhaan ▼
Eupodotis ruficrista
(50 cm) 237

(M)

These **larger ground birds** spend most of their time on the ground, and are only seen flying when threatened or displaying. The **Southern Ground-Hornbills** look like large turkeys, and have a deep, booming call, often heard at dawn. The birds stalk through the veld in pairs or groups looking for snails, frogs, insects, small mammals and reptiles. The **korhaan** is the only species in this group that doesn't roost in trees at night. When threatened it stands still, using camouflage to hide in the bush. The male displays a red crest when courting. It makes distinctive tongue-clicking sounds, then loud, short, piping calls, and often a spectacular, directly upward flight with a 'plummet' back to the ground.

Guineafowl, which gather in flocks, are among our best-loved and noisiest birds, their call also being characteristic of rural Africa. **Francolins** scratch and peck the ground in pairs or small groups for seeds, berries and grubs. Their repeated call – a loud, crowing *'chak, kikwerri-kwetchi'* – is characteristic of the Lowveld at dawn and dusk.

Crested Francolin ►
Dendroperdix sephaena
(32 cm) 189

▲ Helmeted Guineafowl
Numida meleagris (53 - 58 cm) 203

DRIER BUSH

ON OR NEAR THE GROUND

Although these birds are often seen foraging on the ground, many are first spotted in bushes or trees where they escape danger and build their nests. A number of them are a common sight around human habitation. Here they benefit from the shorter grass that exposes seeds and insects and makes food easier to find.

▲ Golden-breasted Bunting
Emberiza flaviventris
(16 cm) 884

The Golden-breasted Bunting is most often seen walking on the ground beneath bushes or trees, foraging for insects and seeds. It is easily recognised by is golden breast and black-and-white striped head. The nest is a cup of grass stems and roots, normally in the fork of a small tree.

Burchell's Starling ►
Lamprotornis australis
(32 cm) 762

▼ Cape Glossy Starlin
Lamprotornis niten
(22 cm) 764

These **starlings** are gregarious and the species intermingle, often becoming very tame around camp. In bright sunlight, they glisten a dark, metallic green, but on a dull, overcast day you will see the splendid subtleties of colour. **Burchell's Starlings** are normally found where trees are taller and denser. **Cape Glossy Starlings** can be a delight, performing aerobatics before roosting at night. They often perch in treetops, making a loud noise (a harsh, high-pitched croaking).

These **doves** forage for seeds and insects on the ground. The **Cape Turtle-Dove** has a thin, black collar round the back of the neck. Males display by flapping straight upward, and then coo-ing while spiralling back down to their perch. Most easily recognised by its pinky, spotted chest, the **Laughing Dove** is a common resident. Males pursue females along a branch or on the ground, with a comic hunched, hopping gait.

▲ Cape Turtle-Dove
Streptopelia capicola
(28 cm) 354

Laughing Dove ►
Streptopelia senegalensis
(25 cm) 355

White-browed
Scrub-Robin ►
Cercotrichas leucophrys
(15 cm) 613
Usually solitary, this robin often hides in tangled scrub. It hops while foraging for insects and spiders, and may flick its tail up and down, especially if alarmed.

◄ Red-billed Hornbill
Tockus erythrorhynchus
(46 cm) 458

The nesting behaviour of both **hornbills** is similar. The females are sealed in a hole in a tree, so that only the beak protrudes. The male feeds the female during this period. After the first egg hatches she breaks out, and the nestlings reseal the opening. Both the **Red-billed** and **Yellow-billed Hornbills'** calls are a very similar *'wak wak wak'* which speeds up into double notes of a duet *'kawak kawak kawak'* and sounds like *'go back go back go back'*.

Southern Yellow-billed
Hornbill ►
Tockus leucomelas
(48 - 60 cm) 459

(M)

These three small birds **are often found in bird parties** and they can become tame around human habitation. They may be seen feeding on the ground in pairs (when breeding) or in small groups. The **Blue Waxbill** is recognised by its delicate blue face and breast. It feeds in small flocks (up to 40), and flies rapidly into dense bush if alarmed.

Blue Waxbill
Uraeginthus angolensis
(13 cm) 844

The bright yellow rump and white-tipped tail of the **Yellow-fronted Canary** identifies it in flight. The males sing a whistling chirp (sometimes together) from a conspicuous perch. The **Red-billed Firefinch** is a remarkable red, with a pink bill. Like the Blue Waxbill, it flies to the nearest cover when disturbed.

▲ Yellow-fronted Canary
(Yellow-eyed Canary)
Crithagra mozambicus
(12 cm) 869

(F)

(M)

Red-billed Firefinch ►
Lagonosticta senegala
(10 cm) 842

Drier Bush

Using Prominent Perches

These birds use prominent perches to spot potential prey. Apart from the fruit-eating Grey Go-away-bird, they are all carnivorous. They tend to 'pounce' on their victims, or catch their prey in flight. Some of them, like the Fork-tailed Drongo, also follow grazing animals or grassfires to catch fleeing insects. Red-billed Oxpeckers are usually spotted clambering about the necks or backs of large mammals, where they eat ticks off the skin. The Grey Go-away-bird is included here as it is often seen on a prominent perch where it warns animals and birds of any danger.

The diet of any bird determines the shape of its beak, or vice versa. Most of these birds have hooked bills to help them hold on to or tear up their prey. The kingfishers have sharp bills, which they use to stab and slice up their prey. The oxpecker uses its slender bill in a scissor-like action to remove parasites.

Grey Go-away-bird ► (Grey Lourie)
Corythaixoides concolor
(49 cm) 373
This large parrot-like bird is one of the characters of the bush, with its well-known, raucous *'Go-away'* call. It eats fruit, leaves, seeds, buds, insects, and even small nestlings. It moves agilely through tree branches, and raises and lowers its crest when alarmed.

◄ Fork-tailed Drongo
Dicrurus adsimilis
(24 cm) 541
Identified by its distinctly forked tail, this dark-black bird is familiar in bushy areas. It is loud and noisy, often mimicking other bird calls. It eats insects, small birds, fish and nectar.

◄ Red-billed Oxpecker
Buphagus erythrorhynchus
(20 - 22 cm) 772
Large mammals, especially buffalo and giraffe, are hosts of the Red-billed Oxpecker. The birds are found in small groups (2 - 6) picking ticks and horseflies off the animal's hide. They are hardly ever found on healthy elephant.

▼ Locust (Grasshopp
Zanocercus eleg
Insect (1 - 11 c
When they swarm these insects are refer to as locusts, but when solitary they are grasshopp Many grasshoppers are eaten by animals and birds. Those with very bright colours, like the one shown here, are distasteful or poisonous, and are avoided by predators.

Shrikes are well known for their rapacious habits and aggressive nature. The **Magpie Shrike** is usually seen in small groups in Acacia savannah, its long tail the characteristic feature. Also found in small groups, or alone, the **Southern White-crowned Shrike** prefers dry woodland or thornveld. The white head and breast are striking.

The **Red-backed Shrike** is an unmistakeable common summer visitor, migrating from Europe and Asia where it breeds. It impales insects and small reptiles on thorns, which serve as a food cache.

▲ Southern White-crowned Shrike
Eurocephalus anguitimens
(24 cm) 756

Magpie Shrike ▲
(Long-tailed Shrike)
Corvinella melanoleuca
(40 - 50 cm) 735

Red-backed Shrike ►
Lanius collurio
(18 cm) 733

Brown-hooded Kingfisher ►
Halcyon albiventris
(23 cm) 435

Striped Kingfisher ►
Halcyon chelicuti
(17 - 19 cm) 437

▼ Lilac-breasted Roller
Coracias caudata
(35 - 36 cm) 447

The remarkable colours of this roller are unmistakeable. It often perches on a bush next to the road, or flies down to seize an insect, such as a grasshopper. Typically of rollers, the courtship display consists of spectacular tumbling aerobatics (mid-winter to early spring).

These two **kingfishers** are actually not fish-eaters, but wait for insects and small lizards to appear on the ground below. They are often found in similar habitats. The **Brown-hooded Kingfisher** nests in a 1-metre-long tunnel in a steep bank, while the **Striped Kingfisher** nests in a hole in a tree. It is smaller, with a white collar and a lower red and upper black bill.

rasshopper

Drier Bush

In the Canopy of Trees

The birds on this page are usually found within the canopy of bushes and trees. As with other animals, birds are specially adapted for a specific food niche. Some forage for fruit, some take insects from leaves and stems, while others search the bark and trunk for caterpillars. The woodpeckers have two toes facing forward and two backward, to provide a good grip on the tree. The hard skull is cushioned by muscles to absorb the impact of continual pecking.

Many birds associate in groups or flocks. This behaviour helps the birds to survive, through increased vigilance and protection.

◄ Red-faced Mousebird
Urocolius indicus
(34 cm) 426

These birds are **gregarious.** The small **Red-faced Mousebird** looks a little like a parrot. It has a crest and a parrot-shaped, fruit-eating beak. Flocks of 5 - 20 birds can be seen creeping and crawling through the vegetation like mice. **Brown-headed Parrots** are often seen in small groups, screeching with typical parrot-like whistles. They clamber about in flowering or fruiting trees, eating fruit, nuts, nectar and seeds. Up to 50 birds can be found together at a good food source.

Brown-headed Parrot ▼
Poicephalus cryptoxanthus
(23 cm) 363

◄ Green Wood-Hoopoe
(Red-billed Woodhoopoe)
Phoeniculus purpureus
(34 cm) 452

Green Wood-Hoopoes are common, noisy birds found in groups of 2 - 16, with one breeding pair in the group. They may be seen examining tree trunks and branches for insects, millipedes and lizards. When calling, they rock back and forth cackling loudly, which is likened to laughing women in the Zulu name *Kehkala.*

(M)

These **two small birds** eat insects, and may join mixed bird parties. The **Southern Black Tit** enjoys caterpillars, which it finds under bark or in seedpods. These birds live in pairs or small groups, and prefer moister habitats. The **Chinspot Batis** can be heard calling constantly '*weep woop*' or '*weep woop wurp*', sounding like 'three blind mice'. It often hangs upside down to remove its prey, frequently spiders, from leaves. It lives alone or in pairs, preferring drier bush.

Southern Black Tit ▲
Parus niger
(16 cm) 554

Chinspot Batis ▼
Batis molitor
(13 cm) 701

(F)

(M)

◄ Golden-tailed Woodpecker
Campethera abingoni
(20 cm) 483

Woodpeckers scurry around dead trees, tapping the wood with their beaks to open up caterpillar tunnels. The sound of tapping on dry wood carries for long distances. The birds usually land low on the tree and work their way upwards. The **Golden-tailed Woodpecker** can be distinguished by the heavy streaking on its cheeks and throat, and the **Cardinal Woodpecker** by its brown forehead.

Marico Sunbird ►
Cinnyris mariquensis
(14 cm) 779

The female of the Marico Sunbird lacks the bright colours of the male, but she has her own delicate beauty. They are found alone or in pairs in Acacia savannah. They use their long, curved beaks to probe nectar from flowers and to catch insects in the air.

Cardinal Woodpecker ►
Dendropicos fuscescens
(15 cm) 486

◄ Woodland Kingfisher
Halcyon senegalensis
(22 - 24 cm) 433

These three species are all common **summer migrants** (October - April) from further north in Africa. Cuckoos parasitise or lay their eggs in the nests of other birds, who then rear the nestlings. The **Woodland Kingfisher** flashes bright light blue, while perching, or flying low in tree canopies. It usually nests in old barbet or woodpecker holes, and eats insects, small reptiles and frogs, and, rarely, fish. The **Diderick Cuckoo** may parasitise weaver and sparrow nests. With its distinctive '*dee-dee-deedereek*' call, it is more often heard than seen. The **Jacobin Cuckoo** parasitises mainly Fork-tailed Drongo and bulbul nests. The male distracts the host so that the female can lay her eggs.

◄ Diderick Cuckoo
Chrysococcyx caprius
(19 cm) 386

Jacobin Cuckoo ▲
Clamator jacobinus
(34 cm) 382

Dense Bush near Water

These birds live in the large trees and dense bush close to rivers. Many of them are also found around camp gardens that have water. They forage in the canopies for fruit and insects, and are therefore difficult to find. Bright colouration, sudden movement or bird calls give them away.

In these moist habitats, there is often a great concentration of birds around flowering and fruiting trees. Many of them enjoy figs and other fruit. They help with germination by partly digesting and softening the seed capsules. Birds that eat flowers and nectar play a vital role in cross-pollination as the pollen sticks to their beaks. The birds are therefore invaluable in the life-cycle of some of the riverine trees.

Walk quietly around camp with a pair of binoculars. You might be able to see a number of birds that you have only been able to hear in the bushes while driving around.

◄ Trumpeter Hornbill
Bycanistes bucinator
(62 cm) 455

The Trumpeter Hornbill and Green-Pigeon are **gregarious and eat fruit,** especially figs. They are often found eating together in fig trees (page 11). The **Trumpeter Hornbill** is a large, fascinating bird with a conspicuous horny ridge (casque) on top of its bill. The casque is hollow, and may be used to amplify the long, trumpet-like calls that sound like a baby crying. The **African Green-Pigeon** hangs upside down like a parrot to reach ripe fruit. Its green plumage provides excellent camouflage within the leafy canopy. While Green-Pigeons only eat fruit, Trumpeter Hornbills also eat large insects.

◄ Black-collared Barbet
Lybius torquatus
(20 cm) 464

A highly vocal bird (especially in summer during breeding), the Black-collared Barbet is recognised by its red head and black collar. Its call is a quickly repeated duet. The male calls *'hoop'* first, immediately followed by the *'pud-duh-ly'* of the female. It eats fruit (especially figs) and insects.

▲ African Green-Pigeon
Treron calva
(30 cm) 361

▼ Purple-crested Turaco
(Purple-crested Lourie)
Gallirex porphyreolophus
(42 cm) 371

Purple-crested Turacos hide in the canopy, running agilely along the branches, foraging for fruit and buds. Their conspicuous crimson wings may be spotted as they glide through thick canopies. They call repeatedly and together *'kok-kok-kok'*, which rises in volume and excitement.

Dark-capped Bulbul ►
(Black-eyed Bulbul)
Pycnonotus tricolor
(22 cm) 568

A lively, liquid call is characteristic of Dark-capped Bulbuls, uttered while foraging for fruit and insects. They are very noisy, territorial birds, and will quickly sound their alarm call, *'chissik chissik'*, when a snake, owl or mongoose is near.

◄ White-bellied Sunbird
Nectarinia talatala
(11 cm) 787

Black-headed Oriole ▼
Oriolus larvatus
(25 cm) 545

This enchanting bird moves in the tops of tall trees, calling in beautiful liquid notes. It eats insects, berries and nectar. The nest hangs hammock-like from a slender branch, and is made of stringy lichen, moss and grass, bound with spider's web.

Sunbirds are often seen around lodges or camps with flowering trees. They eat nectar, which is sucked up with a tube-like tongue, and insects. A nest is made of grass, leaves and other material, bound with spider's web and suspended from a branch of a tree or bush. Although female sunbirds appear drab, the males are spectacular. The male **White-bellied Sunbird** has a unique metallic-green head and throat, with a white belly; the male **Scarlet-chested Sunbird** has a large, diagnostic scarlet chest patch.

Scarlet-chested Sunbird ►
Nectarinia senegalensis
(14 cm) 791

Dense Bush near Water

All these birds eat insects and other small animals. Some of them forage on the ground, while others move through the canopy of trees searching for prey. Except for the ground-nesting Natal Spurfowl, they all build their nests within the tree canopies. The nests are either well-camouflaged, or inaccessible to predators. They are not, however, completely out of danger. Snakes can wind their way up trees and into weaver nests even though they appear well protected.

◄ Burchell's Coucal
Centropus burchellii
(42 cm) 391a

This large bird skulks through vegetation in a reptile-like way. It is also know as the Rain Bird, as its descending, bubbling call is associated with imminent rain. It preys on insects, small frogs, reptiles, nestling birds, and mammals.

(M)

African Paradise-Flycatcher ►
Terpsiphone viridis
(41 cm [M], 23 cm [F]) 710

Common in rest camps, the African Paradise-Flycatcher catches small insects on the wing. The male has incredibly long tail feathers that trail out behind him as he flies. Paradise Flycatchers have a tiny nest bound with spider's web and camouflaged with plant fibres and lichen, usually in the fork of a tree.

(M)

(M display)

▲ Black-backed Puffback
Dryoscopus cubla
(18 cm) 740

Each **shrike** has its own unique, distinctive call. These three hide and crawl through dense vegetation, and are more often heard than seen. The **Black-backed Puffback** also forages high in the trees, seldom venturing lower down. It calls *'chick, weeo'* in loud, repetitive click-whistling notes. During courtship the male puffs up his splendid, gleaming white back or rump feathers. The beautiful **Orange-breasted Bush-Shrike** tends to move in the tops of trees. Its call is like Morse code, in 5 - 8 '*poo-poo-poo-poooo*' notes. The shy **Southern Boubou** keeps to thick undergrowth and lower branches. The males and females call constantly to each other to keep in touch. The duet is variable, with a basic '*boo-boo*' followed by a whistled '*whee-ooo*'.

Orange-breasted Bush-Shrike ►
Telophorus sulfureopectus
(18 - 19 cm) 748

(M)

Southern Boubou ▼
Laniarius ferrugineus
(21 - 23 cm) 736

(M)

◄ **White-fronted Bee-eater**
Merops bullockoides
(24 cm) 443

White-fronted Bee-eaters perch in small groups, waiting for insects to fly past, then agilely hawk them in mid-air, before returning to perch and eat. They nest in 1-metre-long burrows excavated in riverbanks where colonies breed. They breed during months when food, often butterflies, is most abundant.

(Breeding M)

Village Weaver ►
(Spotted-backed Weaver)
Ploceus cucullatus
(15 - 17 cm) 811

Always gregarious, Spotted-backed Weavers nest, forage and bath communally in large flocks. The male builds an oval grass nest, which droops from branches hanging over water. The male may court two or more females when breeding. When the male is unable to attract the female, she will destroy his nest, and he will be forced to rebuild it – often many times.

Natal Spurfowl ►
(Natal Francolin)
Pternistes natalensis
(36 cm) 196

These three birds are **ground foragers in moister areas**. **Natal Spurfowls** can be heard calling at dawn and dusk in a repeated raucous, crowing *'kwadi kwadi kwadi'*. They move in pairs or parties of up to ten, eating snails, insects, roots, fruit and seeds. The **Hadeda Ibis'** call is also a well-loved sound in the Lowveld. They call '*Ha ha...Hadeda*' when disturbed, or when leaving their roosts in the morning. They probe into the ground with their long, curved bills, or peck up insects, snails, reptiles and earthworms. The **Kurrichane Thrush** is usually alone, or in pairs, running in short bursts, and then stopping to peck the ground for insects and lizards.

▲ **Hadeda Ibis**
Bostrychia hagedash
(76 cm) 94

Kurrichane Thrush ►
Turdus libonyana
(22 cm) 576

Open Water

Waterbirds are specifically associated with open water habitats, such as rivers, pans, lakes and dams. As in other habitats, the birds use different niches to eat and breed. Some birds wade in the shallow water, while others swim and dive where it is deeper. Plovers prefer the open ground surrounding the water, and crakes and jacanas are agile on floating water plants. Kingfishers prefer higher vantage points to scan the water for prey.

The open water habitat is one of the easiest places to spot and identify birds, because many are conspicuous and exposed.

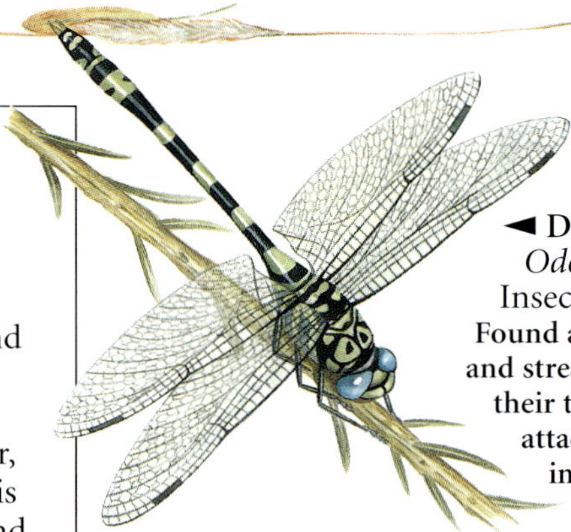

◄ Dragonfly
Odonata species
Insect (4,5 - 14 cm)
Found at the edges of ponds and streams, the males defend their territories by attacking or chasing away intruders. The male and female may be seen flying together in tandem as they mate, occasionally licking the surface of the water so the female can lay her eggs.

Damselfly ▼
Family *Coenagrionidae*
Insect (15 - 50 mm)
The damselfly folds its wings together when resting (the dragonfly holds its wings out horizontally). Like the dragonfly, the damselfly preys on insects, and lays its eggs in water. The adults can be found far from water, where they escape predation and search for prey.

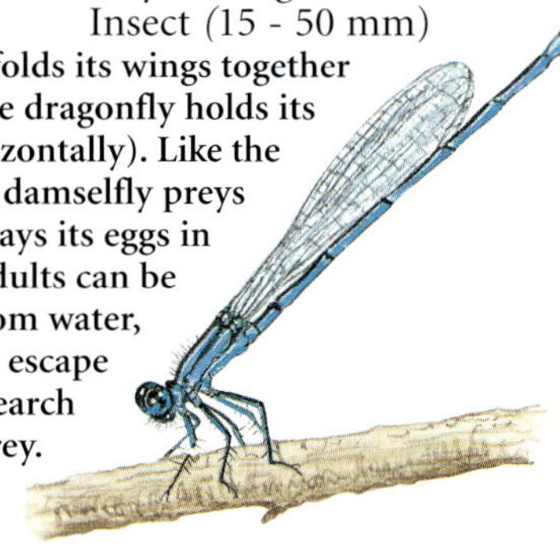

◄ Hamerkop
Scopus umbretta (56 cm) 81
Usually seen alone, the Hamerkop has a conspicuous hammer-shaped head. It may either patrol the shallows for frogs and tadpoles, or snatch morsels from the water surface in flight. It builds a huge, dome-shaped nest (up to 2 metres in diameter) of sticks and reeds in trees, near water.

Blacksmith Lapwing ►
(Blacksmith Plover)
Vanellus armatus (30 cm) 258
Found in pairs or small groups, Blacksmith Lapwings eat and nest on the shorelines of water bodies. They are extremely vocal, 'screeching' when their nest is threatened. The nest is simply an exposed scrape in the soil, but the eggs are well camouflaged.

(M)

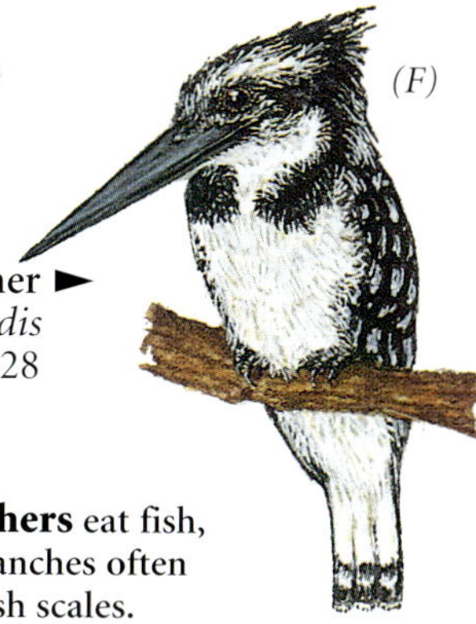

(F)

Giant Kingfisher ▼
Megaceryle maximus
(46 cm) 429

▲ Pied Kingfisher ►
Ceryle rudis
(25 - 29 cm) 428

(M)

Both these **kingfishers** eat fish, their favourite branches often being coated in fish scales. **Giant Kingfishers** perch over water, looking for fish, crabs or frogs within range. **Pied Kingfishers** hover above water with miraculously fast wingbeats, then plunge in head-first, returning to a perch to kill their catch. They also eat shellfish and insects. Both these species nest in tunnels burrowed into river or stream banks.

African Pied Wagtail ►
Motacilla aguimp (20 cm) 711

The black-and-white Pied Wagtail may be seen walking around on rocks or sandbanks, and suddenly chasing or leaping after a crawling or flying insect, such as a dragonfly. It regularly bobs its tail up and down, especially on landing or when agitated. It becomes tame around human habitation.

▼ Black Crake
Amaurornis flavirostris
(21 cm) 213

The bright red legs and eyes of the Black Crake, and its yellow beak, are a striking contrast to the black body. It is usually seen walking over floating vegetation in reedy or marshy areas. Its eerie call can be heard in reedbeds. It eats insects, snails, crabs, worms, small fish, small birds, herons' eggs, seeds and water plants.

African Jacana ▲
Actophilornis africanus
(28 cm) 240

Also known as Lily-trotters, African Jacanas walk on floating plants to move about the water surface hunting for insects, crustaceans and snails (photo pages 34 and 35). They have exceptionally long toes, for balance and to spread their weight. The male looks after the eggs and chicks, carrying them around under his wings, while the female finds her next mate of the season.

Open Water

Waterbirds are all well adapted to their environment. The large wading birds have long legs, giving them a good view of any prey swimming beneath the water surface. Fish-eating birds swallow fish head-first so that the scales and spines are folded flat. Saddle-billed Stork may snip the spines off larger fish before swallowing. Darters, herons and cormorants are often found nesting communally in trees, giving them safety in numbers.

◄ African Fish-Eagle
Haliaeetus vocifer
(63 - 73 cm) 148

This exceptional eagle is usually first noticed as a white patch high in a tree overlooking an expanse of water. It has a magnificent ringing call, given while perching, or circling high overhead. It snatches fish near the water surface with its talons, eating larger ones on the ground, next to the water.

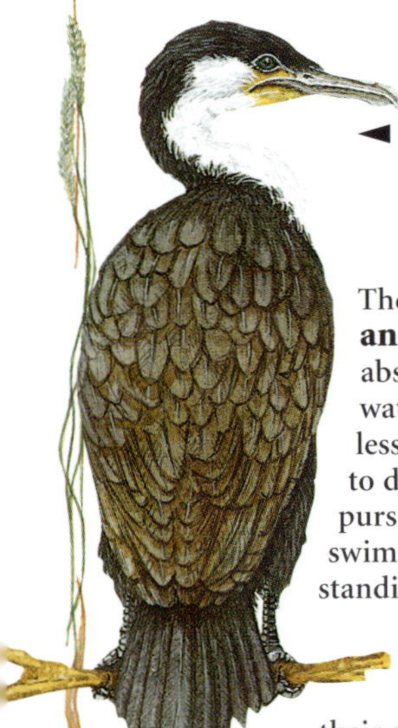

◄ White-breasted Cormorant
Phalacrocorax lucidus
(90 cm) 55

Egyptian Goose ▼
Alopochen aegyptiaca
(70 cm) 102

Very widespread, Egyptian Geese make a great deal of noise before take-off, and during flight. The female 'honks' rapidly, '*honk-haah-haah-haah-haah*', while the male hisses. They eat aquatic plants, grass and seedlings. Pairs mate for life, but when not breeding they gather in large groups on sandbanks.

These two birds **dive for fish and frogs**. Their feathers absorb more water than other water birds. This makes them less buoyant, and enables them to dive deep into the water in pursuit of their prey. After swimming they are often seen standing on rocks or stumps, holding their wings out to dry. **Cormorants** cement their nest together with their guano. They often use the same nest of sticks year after year. **Darters** are also known as 'snake birds' because their kinked necks appear snake-like when they swim. They spear their prey with dagger-like beaks.

◄ African Darter
Anhinga rufa
(79 cm) 60

(Breeding M)

(M)

Saddle-billed Stork ►
Ephippiorhynchus senegalensis (1,4 m) 88
The Saddle-billed Stork is a huge, impressive bird with a bright yellow, red and black bill. The male has brown eyes and a yellow wattle. The female has yellow eyes and no wattle. Seen on its own or in pairs, this shy bird either walks slowly through shallow water looking for prey, or stands and waits for large fish, frogs and crabs to swim within range.

Goliath Heron ▼
Ardea goliath
(1,4 m) 64

Grey Heron ►
Ardea cinerea
(1 m) 62

Both **solitary birds**, these herons stand in shallow water for long periods, waiting for a passing fish, which they snap up with their long sharp bills. They also eat frogs, insects, reptiles, small mammals and birds. They build a platform of sticks on trees or in reedbeds.
The **Goliath Heron** usually nests alone, only occasionally with other herons. The **Grey Heron** roosts and nests communally.

Green-backed Heron ▼
Butorides striatus (40 cm) 74
This small, squat heron prefers denser vegetation. It is shy and solitary, and skulks around reeds and branches. It stands still for long periods, in a typical hunched posture, waiting for fish and frogs. It is unique in using bait such as live insects, as well as twigs, leaves and feathers, to lure fish within range of its dagger-like bill.

Raptors and Scavengers

Raptors (birds of prey) and scavengers are all carnivorous birds. They have hooked bills for tearing apart animal flesh, and large talons for seizing and holding their prey. Vultures mostly scavenge on dead animals. They fly masterfully, using the thermal updrafts for soaring and gliding at great heights in search of carcasses far below. These large birds nest in the tops of trees, or in forks of large trees. The nest is a platform of sticks, and many birds return year after year to re-use the same nest. Vultures lay only one egg, but most eagles lay two. A few days after hatching, the strongest chick of some eagles usually kills the weaker one. By laying two eggs, the parents increase their chances of successfully raising a strong chick.

Pesticides and herbicides used in agriculture affect the survival of these birds. The poison enters the food chain. This results in fragile eggshells which break before the embryo has a chance to develop. Often no young survive.

Martial Eagle ▲
Polemaetus bellicosus
(78 cm) 140
The largest African Eagle, the Martial Eagle, eats birds, mammals and reptiles (especially monitors – pages 31 and 33). It has astonishing eyesight that enables the bird to spot prey at great distances. It then swoops down in a shallow dive to seize the prey with its massive talons.

◄ Wahlberg's Eagle
Aquila wahlbergi
(58 cm) 135
A very common, small, brown, summer migrant, Wahlberg's Eagles may be seen on nests in large trees along riverbanks. They spen winter in equatorial Africa, and often return to th same nest site (August to April). They are attracted to veld fires, where they catch and eat fleeing insects, reptile and small mammals.

◄ Tawny Eagle
Aquila rapax (69 cm) 132
Tawny Eagles are often seen at carcasses, feeding on carrion. However they are also efficient hunters, and are partial to termites as well. They catch birds in flight and also pirate other birds' food. They may occupy the same nest and territory year after year, when the food supply is good.

◄ **Lizard Buzzard**
Kaupifalco monogrammicus (36 cm) 154

The Lizard Buzzard is easily identified by the diagnostic vertical black streak running down its throat. It is a small grey, nomadic buzzard, preferring broad-leafed woodlands, but also found in savannah. It is often seen perching conspicuously on a tree, from where it searches the ground for insects and lizards.

(M)

Bateleur ►
Terathopius ecaudatus
(63 cm) 146

The striking Bateleur has a characteristic rocking flight, but glides effortlessly on thermals during hot days. In flight it is also easy to recognise by its contrast of black and white, and because it appears almost tail-less. It eats mostly small mammals and birds, but also reptiles, fish, carrion and eggs. Immature Bateleurs take 7 - 8 years to change their youthful brown plumage to full adult colours.

◄ **Hooded Vulture**
Necrosyrtes monachus
(65 - 75 cm) 121

Vultures are scavengers, cleaning up carcasses and preventing the spread of disease. They have bald or sparsely haired heads, an adaptation to the bloody feeding conditions. The small **Hooded Vulture** cannot compete with larger vultures at the carcass. It usually arrives first at a kill, and moves off when the larger vultures arrive. It picks up the scraps on the side, or those left behind. It also feeds on insects that it digs with its slender beak from dung or soil. The **White-backed Vulture** is also one of the first vultures to arrive at a carcass, often following carnivores, crows and kites to locate food. **Lappet-faced Vultures** usually dominate carcasses, and can tear open tough skin with their massive bills, when other vultures do not have the strength.

ite-backed
Vulture ►
os africanus
(94 cm) 123

▲ **Lappet-faced Vulture**
Aegypius tracheliotus
(102 cm) 124

NIGHT CREATURES

The diversity of animals seen during the day is matched by those that move around at night. Many of these animals are common, but they are seldom seen because of their nocturnal habits. They are well adapted to a nocturnal lifestyle. Some have very large eyes to capture as much light as possible, while others compensate with excellent hearing or smell.

Nocturnal animals can live together by using different parts of the same habitat. Some, such as the bushbabies, are arboreal (living above the ground). Others, such as the genets, are semi-arboreal, while others are entirely terrestrial (living on the ground), like the White-tailed Mongoose. The animals also have different diets, which reduces competition for food.

The following night creatures are featured – mammals (including bats), birds, insects and their relatives (the scorpions and Red Roman). The large carnivores, such as the lion, leopard and hyaena are illustrated on page 21 because of their greater daytime visibility.

Mammals are measured in height H - ground to shoulder, or in length L - tip of nose to tip of tail; birds from beak-tip to tail-tip; bats and moths by their wingspan.

The Spotted Eagle-Owl (page 61) is a very successful nocturnal carnivorous bird.

Nocturnal Carnivores

These carnivores are active when night falls. However, some of them, like the serval, also move around at dawn and dusk. The smaller carnivores are infrequently seen, and are less well known than the larger ones. Carnivores differ considerably in size, colour markings and behaviour, and are fascinating to spot. They try to avoid one another, to prevent competition and potential conflict that may end in death. The smaller species shelter and hide in holes in the ground, in dense vegetation, or up trees to protect themselves. The large ones depend on their strength and size for survival.

As already mentioned, animals tend to fill specific niches. Some are very selective in their habitat requirements, such as the serval, which needs an adequate water supply and some form of cover. Others, like the caracal, are very adaptable and can survive under diverse habitat conditions. As a consequence of being adaptable, generalists often compete with many other species.

◄ Small-spotted Genet
Genetta genetta
(L: 95 cm; 1,8 - 2 kg)

These animals are **mostly solitary, and have a similar diet** of reptiles, frogs, birds, insects, small mammals and fruit. Genets are very agile climbers and spend much time in trees. The white-tipped tail of the **Small-spotted Genet** distinguishes it from the Large-spotted Genet *(Genetta tigrina)*. The animals' colour markings may confuse identification, but the **African Civet** is terrestrial and is far larger than the genets, with a shorter tail. Secretions from the civet's anal glands were once used in perfumes.

▲ African Civet
Civettictis civetta
(L: 1,2 - 1,4 m; 11 - 12 kg)

◄ White-tailed Mongoose
Ichneumia albicauda
(L: 1 m; 4,2 kg)

The White-tailed Mongoose is mostly solitary, although sometimes seen in family groups, and inhabits woodland savannah. It hunts by smell and hearing, using its long front claws to dig up prey. It eats mostly insects, and sometimes birds, reptiles and small mammals. This species may be confused with Meller's Mongoose *(Rhynchogale melleri)* as it also has a white tail. However Meller's has a brown body, and never appears black, as does the White-tailed Mongoose.

Caracal ►
Felis caracal
(L: 1 - 1,2 m; 7 - 19 kg)
A secretive and solitary animal, the caracal is seldom seen. It is recognised by its distinctively long, black ear tufts. It prefers open savannahs and rocky areas, where it is an agile climber and formidable predator. It hunts anything from insects to small antelope.

African Wild Cat ►
Felis lybica
(L: 0,8 - 1 m; 4 - 5 kg)
The African Wild Cat is similar to a domestic cat in behaviour and expression. It is mostly solitary except when breeding, and can hunt large prey such as dassies, rabbits or even the young of small antelope. Interbreeding with domestic cats threatens Wild Cat populations.

◄ Serval
Felis serval
(L: 0,9 - 1,2 m; 8 - 13 kg)
The serval has long legs and large ears with white patches, and prefers savannahs with grass cover. It uses its large ears to locate small rodents and birds in thick grass, and then captures them with a characteristic curved, leaping pounce. It is sometimes seen in the late afternoon and early morning.

Other Nocturnal Animals

These fascinating nocturnal mammals fill a different niche in the night-life world, feeding on plants and insects. They often fall prey to carnivores, and defend themselves in diverse ways. Porcupines walk backwards rattling their sharp quills, while bushbabies leap about in tree canopies. The Scrub Hares lie in the grass with their big ears flattened against their heads. All these animals are part of the food chain that keeps the system alive.

Night-life offers another world of experience, full of new sounds, smells and excitement. A wandering spotlight will pick out the shining eyes of animals actively going about their nocturnal business.

Thick-tailed Bushbaby ►
Otolemur crassicaudatus
(L: 70 - 80 cm; 1,1 kg)

Bushbabies live in trees, and are very agile, leaping 2 - 3 metres across branches. They wipe urine on their feet and hands to scent-mark their territory. Bushbabies are preyed on by genets (page 56) and owls (page 61). They forage alone for gum, fruit and insects, but sleep in family groups. The **Thick-tailed Bushbaby** lives in well wooded areas, while the **Lesser Bushbaby** prefers the savannah (especially Acacia). The Thick-tailed Bushbaby has a call like a crying baby.

◄ Lesser Bushbaby
Galago moholi
(L: 30 - 40 cm; 170 g)

▲ Transvaal Thick-tailed Scorpion
Parabuthus transvaalicus
(up to 14 cm)

The tail and pincer size of a **scorpion** can indicate if the animal is venomous or not. The **Thick-tailed Scorpion** has a thick tail, slender pincers, and is dangerous to humans. It stings its prey, affecting the nervous system which causes paralysis or death. The **Shiny Burrowing Scorpion** has a slender tail and large pincers, which give a painful but not deadly sting. Both scorpions are active at night. During the day, the dangerous Thick-tailed species hides under stones, rocks or dead logs, while the Shiny Burrowing Scorpion burrows into the ground up to 1 metre deep.

▲ Shiny Burrowing Scorpi
Opistophthalmus glabrif
(5 - 12 cm)

▼ Red Roman (Solifuge)
Family *Solifugae* (2 - 5 cm)
This nocturnal, spider-like creature is non-venomous, does not produce silk, and belongs to a group called the Solifuges. It can be identified by its large, formidable jaws used for killing prey, and the leg-like appendages in front (pedipalps), which give it the appearance of having ten legs.

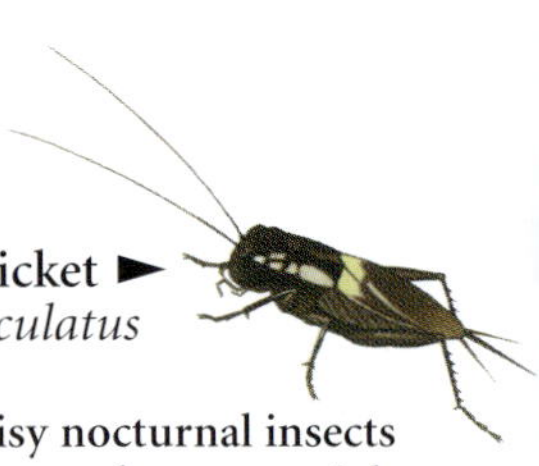

Common Cricket ►
Gryllus bimaculatus
(2,8 cm)
These very noisy nocturnal insects will be heard around camp at night, when they emerge from hiding to feed. The chirping is made by males rubbing their forewings together to attract the females.

Scrub Hare ▼

pus saxatilis (L: 55 cm; 2 kg)
ub Hares live in open savannah
with good grass cover. They are
en spotted darting ahead
car lights at night. They
grass, and will even eat
eir own pellets to extract
all nutrients. They do not
ig burrows but use dense
grass cover for shelter.

Pangolin ▲

Manis temminckii (L: 1,1 m; 7 - 10 kg)
The pangolin forages alone for termites and ants, using its large front claws to tear open termite mounds. It is covered in an armour of heavy scales and, in the same way as a hedgehog, rolls itself up into a protective ball to defend itself.

Aardvark (Antbear) ►

Orycteropus afer
(L: 1,4 - 1,8 m; 40 - 70 kg)
The aardvark uses its strong, bear-like claws and 30-cm-long, sticky tongue to prey on ants and termites. The excavated termite mounds later become burrows for many animals such as hyaena, warthog, and even bats and owls. The aardvark has very poor eyesight, but uses its keen senses of smell and hearing to locate food.

◄ Porcupine

Hystrix africaeaustralis
(L: 0,7 - 1 m; 10 - 24 kg)
The porcupine is Africa's largest rodent. It travels up to 20 km at night, foraging for bark, roots, bulbs and wild fruit. The impressive spines are hollow modified hairs which the porcupine raises and vibrates to ward off predators. Lion and leopard can be fatally injured if quills lodge in their paws or face, making hunting or feeding impossible.

Nocturnal Birds and Bats

The night fliers – both birds and bats – use yet another part of the ecosystem and its habitats. Bats are seen fluttering around at dusk, when they leave their daytime roosts to forage at night. All insect-eating bats use echolocation to catch their prey. They produce pulses of sound, which bounce back from objects near their flight path. The bats pick up the returning echoes to determine the movement of any potential prey. The fruit bats, on the other hand, use their excellent senses of smell and sight to find food. Birds use their sharp eyes and ears to spot prey, swooping down to land on the prey, or snatching it from the air.

The night birds are fascinating, with very distinct, separate calls. Once the calls are known the birds can be easily identified by visitors sitting around the campfire at night.

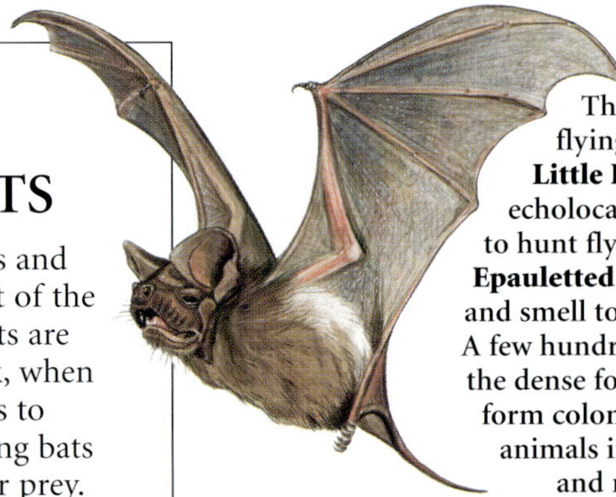

These two **bats** can be seen flying around at dusk. The **Little Free-tailed Bat** uses echolocation for navigation and to hunt flying insects. **Peter's Epauletted Fruit-bat** uses eyesight and smell to find its diet of ripe fruit A few hundred may roost together in the dense foliage of trees. These bats form colonies of a hundred or more animals in caves, roofs of houses and mines.

▲ Little Free-tailed Bat
Tadarida pumila
(L: 9 cm; 11,5 g)

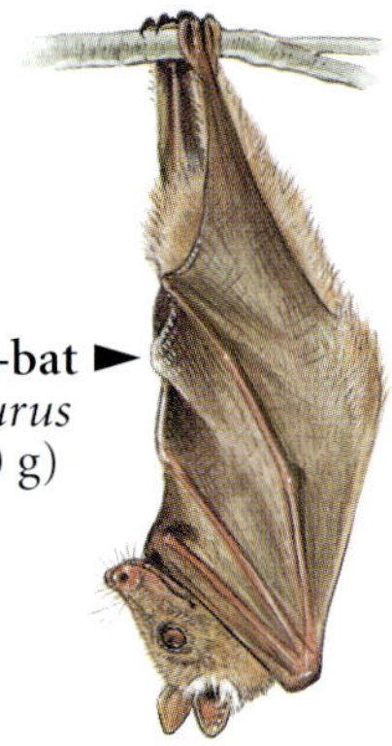

Peter's Epauletted Fruit-bat ►
Epomophorus crypturus
(L: 14 cm; 80 - 140 g)

◄ Spotted Thick-knee
(Spotted Dikkop)
Burhinus capensis
(44 cm) 297

Water Thick-knee ▲
(Water Dikkop)
Burhinus vermiculatus
(38 - 40 cm) 298

These three **long-legged, ground-based birds** shelter in the bushes during the day, and appear at night to forage on insects – the dikkops also eat crustaceans and molluscs. The **Spotted Thick-knee** is found in open savannah. The **Water Thick-knee** lives near water, and is recognised by its conspicuous grey wing-bar. When disturbed, dikkops run with their heads held low. The characteristic night-time calls are similar – a piping *'ti ti ti ti'* rising in pitch and volume, then dying down to a *'tee tee'*. The plover-like **Bronze-winged Courser**, with its red legs, is often spotted on the roads at night. They may freeze, or fly a short distance, to escape the intrusion.

◄ Bronze-winged Courser
Rhinoptilus chalcopterus
(25 cm) 303

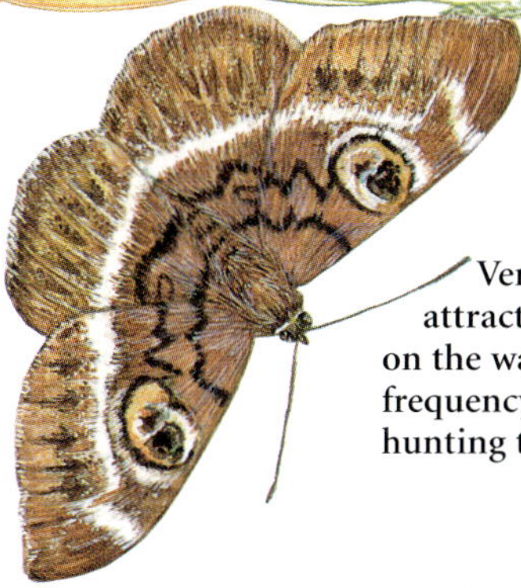

◄ Cream-striped Owl Moth
Cycligramma latona
Insect (wingspan: 62 mm)

Very common, Cream-striped Owl Moths are attracted to artificial light, and may be seen resting on the walls of houses. They can hear the high-frequency sounds insectivorous bats emit when hunting them, and thus avoid being caught.

The **eagle owls** are the largest owls in Africa, and the **Verreaux's Eagle-Owl** is the largest of all. The latter can be identified by its pink eyelids, and makes a distinctive, grunt-like hooting call. Its diet consists of mammals as big as Vervet Monkeys (page 26), birds (including raptors), reptiles, frogs and fish. The **Spotted Eagle-Owl** has distinctive yellow eyes and conspicuous ear tufts, and calls a typical hooting *'hu hoo'*. It eats mostly mice and insects, but also other animals (photo pages 54 and 55).

▲Verreaux's Eagle-Owl
(Giant Eagle Owl)
Bubo lacteus
(60 - 65 cm) 402

◄ Spotted Eagle-Owl
Bubo africanus
(47 cm) 401

Pearl-spotted Owlet ►
Glaucidium perlatum
(18 - 19 cm) 398

One of the smallest owls in southern Africa, the Pearl-spotted Owlet is often seen or heard in the day. It has a distinctive, long, repetitive, whistle-like call, ascending *'tiu tiu tiu tiu tiu'*, then descending, *'teeu teeu teeu'*. It hunts insects, rodents, reptiles, birds up to dove-size, and bats. It has two dark spots, or mock eyes, on the back of its head to confuse predators as to which way it is facing.

Fiery-necked Nightjar ▼
Caprimulgus pectoralis (24 cm) 405

he Fiery-necked Nightjar is often seen roosting or esting on the ground. It is very well camouflaged, s long, pointed wings, and flies silently as it hawks sects from the air. It calls *'good lord'* in an initial rising whistle, ending in a series of falling trills *'deliver us'*.

HUMAN HISTORY

The savannah country of the Lowveld and its nearby mountain ranges have a diverse human history. Over millennia it has been home to a variety of races, including the Stone Age San, Bantu-speaking farmers, and the early traders, gold-diggers and settlers from Europe.

The lush vegetation and plentiful game of the subtropical Lowveld have supported a growing human population over thousands of years. However, searing heat and pests such as Tsetse Fly and mosquito brought quick death to many of the traders, hunters and prospectors who ventured into the area in more recent times.

Braving the area's unforgiving climate and wild exterior, many strong and determined people survived to exploit its significant riches. The legacy of their creative and inventive spirit is evident in both ancient and contemporary ruins and preserved sites scattered across the Lowveld.

*Further reading: A Beginners Guide – **Images of Power** by David Lewis-Williams and Thomas Dowson; Field Guide to Rock Art – **Fragile Heritage** by David Lewis-Williams and Geoffrey Blundell.*

Spotting humans can be fun too – from the bonnet of a 1940s Chevrolet!

Early History

The early human history of the Lowveld has been overshadowed by its later history of European exploration and settlement. Archaeological work has, however, uncovered undisputable and fascinating evidence of civilisation thousands of years before the arrival of people from other lands and continents.

Stone and Iron Age peoples roamed the area, hunting, gathering and eventually planting crops, and forging iron. Theirs is a history integral to the Lowveld – as rich and varied as the area itself.

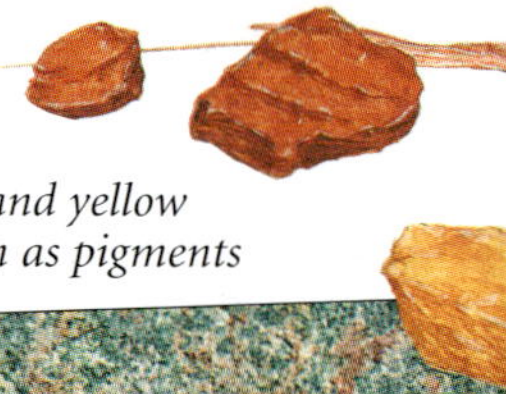

Fragments of red and yellow ochre, used by the San as pigments

San rock painting found in the Lowve

San bow and poison-tipped arrow

Deadliest Euphorbia
Euphorbia cooperi

The Stone Age

One and a half million years ago ancient humans (*Homo erectus*) roamed the Lowveld, scavenging, foraging, and hunting the prehistoric ancestors of the elephant, the giraffe and the baboon.

By the Later Stone Age (beginning 40 000 years ago), nomadic hunter-gatherers known as the San were living here. They were skilful hunters, and made a variety of weapons and implements from bone, flint and animal skin. Hunting became easier once poison was used on arrow heads. The poison was made from the Poison Bush, some Euphorbia trees, and the venom of snakes and spiders. It is now believed that these discoveries made it possible to hunt larger game, and gave humans more time to develop spiritually and culturally.

The San were artists and inventors, with strong spiritual beliefs and rituals that connected them intimately with the land and with the spirit world. Rock paintings depict this relationship. They were painted with feathers, fingers and brushes, which the San made from animal hair.

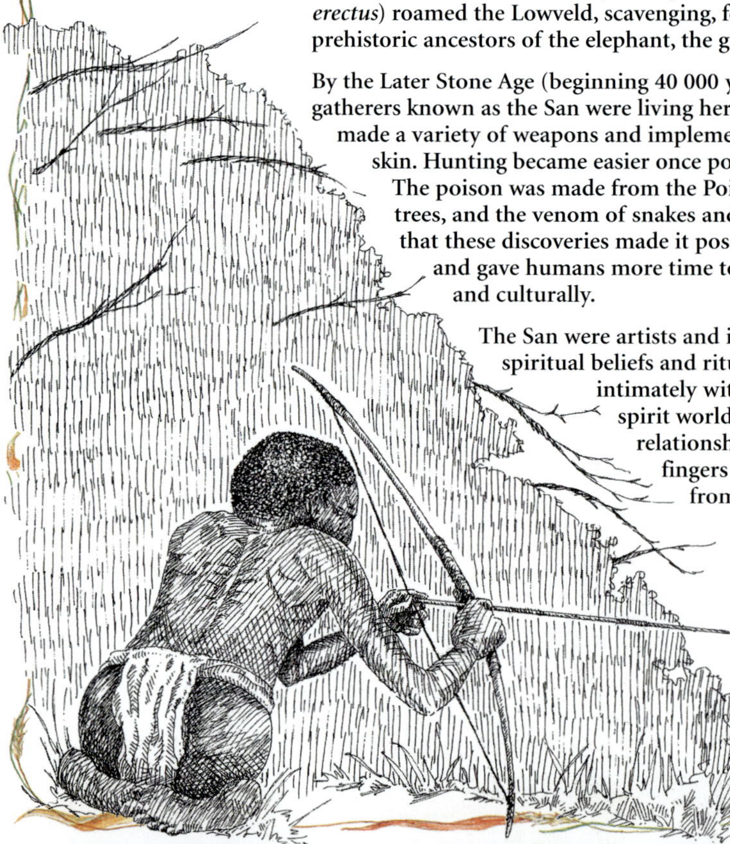

A San hunt

idence of the San's existence over thousands of years can be seen in the many gravings, rock paintings, tools and weapons that have been excavated and preserved sites all around the Lowveld.

Rock painting of a San woman with a digging stick

Iron Age smelting oven

is gold rhino dates to Iron Age

The Iron Age

For centuries, the San lived without competition for resources. But from 200 AD, Bantu-speaking farmers began migrating to the area from central Africa, bringing with them domestic animals and a knowledge of metal-work.

is marked the beginning of the Iron Age in southern Africa. The wcomers mined and worked metal such as iron and copper, and were le to extract gold from the surrounding rock to make ornaments. The ountain caves abundant in the area provided shelter for Iron Age people. one such cave outside Lydenburg, remains of clay masks, probably used for igious or initiation ceremonies, and carbon-dated to 500 AD, have been found.

e now-famous Sudwala Caves were once the retreat of Swazi renegades, hiding from ding groups sent by the Swazi monarch. Surviving members of the renegades were by an officer named Sudwala. He introduced the wonders of the caves to the st Europeans to reach the area, and it is after him that the caves are named.

n Age people also practised simple agriculture, planting ps, such as sorghum and beans, and keeping sheep, tle and goats. Their wattle and mud hut settlements re common along the banks of the many Lowveld ers. By the 15th Century many Bantu-speaking mers had migrated to the area, forcing the nter-gatherer San to retreat further south.

The Marula, Sclerocarya birrea, can indicate early settlements as it was sacred to many tribes, and highly prized for its uses. The young plants would have been nurtured, and the trees would have been protected from fire and from being chopped down (page 3).

Trading and European Settlement

The Mpumalanga Lowveld did not lend itself to easy penetration or settlement. Dense bush, intense heat, malaria-carrying mosquitoes and the dreaded Tsetse Fly, along with wild predators, made this a challenging frontier for even hardened and experienced foreign travellers.

Although traders from the north-east of the continent visited the area before Europeans arrived, it was the breakaway Voortrekkers from the Cape who eventually conquered and claimed much of the Lowveld for settlement.

Glass beads

Trade

Many believe that international trade in southern Africa began with the arrival of the Europeans. However, trade in the area was taking place 1 000 years before the discovery of gold on the Witwatersrand. The Lowveld attracted Arab traders from seaports on the east African coast. They came in search of "white gold" or elephant ivory, and in the Later Iron Age "black gold" – slave labour.

Trade in iron artefacts, glass beads, ivory, bronze, gold and copper gave rise to royal kingdoms and inland trade centres, such as Great Zimbabwe. In the Lowveld, there are stone ruins of such centres at Thulamela, and Matevekvhele, near Punda Maria. At Masorini, near Phalaborwa, iro tools and weapons were manufacture well into the 19th Century.

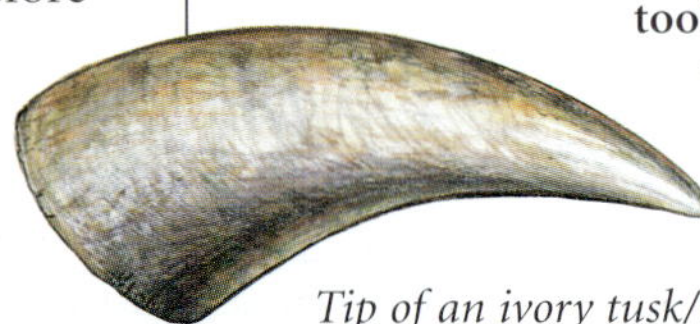

Tip of an ivory tusk/horn

Stone remains at Thulame

Voortrekkers experienced great difficulties and hardships on their journey into the interior.

Broken axle on oxwagon – and 90 miles from nearest blacksmith!

Devil's Thorn (Dicerocaryum eriocarpum) was used as soap and shampoo.

As its name indicates, the Wild Cotton plant (Gossypium herbaceum) was used to make cotton.

ropean settlement

e return of the Cape Colony to British rule in 1806, the subsequent introduction of high ation, and finally the abolition of slavery in 1835, created much resentment among the tch settlers in the Colony. This resulted in what is today known as the Great Trek. Some 00 people (about half the farming population in the Cape) set out on an arduous journey to ntiers north of the Orange River, in hopes of establishing separate Voortrekker Republics.

ong the areas that were eventually settled by these Dutch farmers (Boers) was what is today Mpumalanga Lowveld. For the Boers to escape dependence on the British, it was imperative them to find the ancient African trade routes through this area to the east coast.

he process, these pioneers came up against the perils of the unforgiving environment, own as "the white man's grave", because of the many European explorers who had died while empting to penetrate it.

laria, Tsetse Fly, wild animals, crocodile-infested rivers, and rough and treacherous terrain ravaged st groups of explorers and settlers who ventured into the area. Records describe some of the perils the neers faced:

"As we penetrated deeper into the Lowveld our animals suffered grievously from Tsetse Fly, mosquitoes and ticks. At night, lions prowled the darkness around the camp, shattering the stillness with their roaring, and carried off much of the stock."

Against all odds, Voortrekkers, led by the likes of Andries Potgieter and Andries Pretorius, survived, and claimed much of the interior for European settlement.

example of toys made Voortrekkers: agon (jaw e) and oxen uckle bones)

ng Tom Pass (as it looks day) was one of many that Voortrekkers to negotiate with their oxwagons.

Gold Rush

The discovery of gold in the Lowveld brought a temporary boom to the area. From 1873, hordes of fortune-seeking prospectors descended on places such as Barberton and Pilgrim's Rest to pan the rivers and excavate the reefs for gold. The area was temporarily a hive of activity.

Barberton

Barberton in particular enjoyed a lively career as a centre of wild speculation, gambling and frenetic nightlife. Canteens, music halls and liquor shops competed with the mines for the biggest profits. At the height of its boom, two stock exchanges traded round the clock in the town. On the Sheba Ridge overlooking Barberton lie the ruins of one of the many digging towns – Eureka City. These diggings produced one of the highest yields in the history of gold mining – over 500 000 ounces in ten years.

Gold-digging sp

Barberton cableway carrying gold from the diggi

Further north, African prospectors were mining copper and iron in the remains of an ancient volcanic shaft. This 19-square-kilometre area also hosted such minerals as phosphates, zinc, mica and gold. The prospectors named the place Phalaborwa ("better than the south"), because it was healthier than the fever-ridden areas in the south.

Gold nuggets

Fortune-seeker the late 1800 digging and panning for g

Life in Pilgrim's Rest in the late 1800s

he Lowveld goldrush brought an assortment of unusual characters to the area. Hunters, ivory poachers, prospectors and transport riders abounded, each looking to profit from the discovery of gold. Men such as Sir Percy Fitzpatrick (later a statesman and politician) and his transport riders carried supplies from the east coast through Tsetse Fly-infested bush to the gold-digging areas of the Lowveld.

Tsetse Fly

"They travelled through the worst areas at night, when the fly was less active. They smeared their draught animals with grease and potent mixtures ... and used exotic creatures such as camels in the vain hope that they would prove resistant to the disease."

With the discovery of vast gold deposits on the Witwatersrand in the late 1800s, most prospectors left the Lowveld, and the mining industry in the area declined. The demand for wood for the Highveld mines, however, was to create the next boom industry – forestry, which along with fruit farming has been the economic mainstay of the area ever since.

A trading store of the past, which can be visited today

Kiaat Bloodwood (Wild Teak) (Pterocarpus angolensis) was used for its timber

A saw from the early forestry industry

Conservation

The history of the Sabi-Sand area and the greater Kruger National Park is a story of the perseverance and bravery of many individuals.

Paul Kruger's dream of preserving the wildlife as part of the national heritage was fulfilled through the vision and determination of individuals such as James Stevenson-Hamilton. In the end it took place at the expense of many of the original inhabitants of the area. The Kruger Park has led the way in the development of one of the finest game parks in the world, with a globally respected conservation policy.

Sabi-Sand Area

As far back as the 1860s the Sabi-Sand area was attracting big-game hunters, particularly in the dry winter season when the threat of mosquito and Tsetse Fly diminished. Over the next several decades, the lure of ivory, meat, hides and even hunting trophies began the steady decline of game in the area.

One observer wrote at this time that *"if sportsmen want to 'do' Africa, they had better make haste, as at the present rate of decrease, in a very few years [wild anima will have ceased to exist in this territory."*

Long before the turn of the century the quagga had been hunted into extinction. The protection of the species was only legislated in 1886, three years after the last animal had died in a zoo in Europe. Giraffe were also hunted in abundance, their hides used to make "riems" to span the oxen that drove the most popular form of transport at the time, the wagon.

Spent cartridges

A hunter and his work, 180

Lee-Enfield .303 rifle used by game hunters in the 1800s

Hunting lion

Large-scale hunting continue unabated until the late 1800 The few conservation laws i place did not protect the species, but rather limite the categories of peopl permitted to hunt. Th had grave consequenc for the indigenous subsistence hunters of the area, who were suddenly considered poachers under the law a thus forced into cattle farming. This caus severe ecological damage to the land.

1894, President of the Transvaal Paul
ıger publicly expressed concern
ɔut the slaughter of wildlife for
nmercial gain, and suggested that the
ıe was near to set aside a sanctuary
which game may find refuge."

e political upheavals between Boer
l British over the next decade meant
ıt very little was done to act upon
ıger's "concern". In the mid 1890s,
area between the Sabie and
ɔcodile Rivers was identified as being
table for game preservation, as
laria and horsesickness prevented
ɔlonged human settlement. The Sabie
me Reserve was to be proclaimed a
vernment game reserve, but the onset
the Boer War distracted the attention
legislators, and hunting continued in the area.

The official opening of the Selati railway line, 1912

venson-Hamilton
a young man

The end of the Boer War in 1902 saw the appointment of James Stevenson-Hamilton as warden for the Sabie Game Reserve. He set about trying to get the area officially proclaimed a wildlife reserve, and engaged in protracted negotiations with the various private individuals and companies who owned vast tracts of the land. These people considered the new reserve a threat to their lucrative agricultural plans.

Stevenson-Hamilton persisted in this pursuit for over two decades, under great pressure from the landowners in the area. In 1923 the reserve's borders were redrawn as a compromise to the farmers. Over half a million acres of land, including what is today the heart of the Sabi-Sand Wildtuin, was "released" and fell outside the borders of the reserve.

Rail travel into the area became popular in the early 1920s, with South African Railways promoting a nine-day trip through Nelspruit, Sabie, Tzaneen and on through the reserve to Komatipoort. Game viewing from the comfort of a rail coach was now possible, and public awareness of the beauty of the reserve was increased.

Kruger National Park was officially proclaimed in parliament in 1926 and a Parks Board established
un it. Today it is one of the most famous game reserves in the world, and hosts almost a million
itors every year.

Animals like giraffe (page 18) now had a place of refuge.

An early game-viewing enthusiast to the Kruger National Park

ULUSABA

Ulusaba forms part of the Sabi-Sand Reserve, which is a 66 000 ha privately owned reserve within the greater Kruger National Park. Some of the land has been in private hands since the mid-1800s, and the area was heavily hunted for commercial gain until the early 20th Century. Cattle were introduced by farmers in the 1920s, and by 1927 there were many herds competing with game for grazing.

COURANT

SCHE REPUBLIEK.

Proclamatie door ZHEd. den Staatspresident.

GOUVERNEMENTS-WILDTUIN.

GOD BEHOEDE LAND EN VOLK.

S. J. P. KRUGER, Staatspresident.

Dr. W. J. LEYDS, Staatssecretaris.

The Sabi-Sand Reserve proclamation

Ulusaba

The name Ulusaba, meaning "place of little fear" in Shangaan, was probably given by the Shangaan tribe who have lived in this area for over 200 years. They used the hills as military outposts for their chiefs and senior warriors.

During times of war they were at a great advantage as they could see the enemy advancing from a great distance, so a surprise attack was almost impossible. The tribe thus lived in relative safety.

As European explorers and mine prospectors moved into the Lowveld, Ulusaba and the surrounding area became attractive for altogether different reasons.

Shangaan spear

Young Shangaan women

Game viewing in modern times

The large trees on the river are important landmarks. The huge Sycomore Fig (page 11) that grows on the riverbank at Kirri Crossing is called the Postman's Tree. Post was deposited there once a week between 1900 and 1925, for collection by local farmers along the river.

1893 construction gan on the Selati lway line to link the dfields in the west h the coast. It is said t for every sleeper laid, e man died of fever ring the construction the line. Remnants of railway can still be n at the south end of Ulusaba reserve.

wever, by the time the e was completed in 12, very little gold was ng mined in the Selati d fields. To make the lway profitable, the train r of the Lowveld and zambique was begun.

ring the 1920s the Ulusaba area was stocked with cattle. Predators were an obvious eat to livestock, and between 1927 and 1933 500 lions were shot. In 1938 a t-and-mouth epidemic broke out, and all the cattle were shot.

saba today is sited on the farms Wallingford and Exeter, which were originally ned by Mr L Rattray. He and other landowners in the area adopted the name i-Sand Wildtuin, and agreed on a preservation policy for the reserve in the 1940s.

e Sabi-Sand Reserve was proclaimed a private nature reserve in 1965. By this time nce had been erected between the reserve and the Kruger National Park to combat t-and-mouth disease. The fence was removed in 1993, allowing game to move ely, and for ancient east-west migration routes to be re-established. Ownership of Ulusaba property has changed several times, and most recently the area was ght by a foreign investor with a strong commitment to eco-tourism.

Smaller creatures are also conserved, like the African Leopard butterfly (page 12).

Guests at Ulusaba today on a game drive

Gameviewing Journal

You can't plan a day – it just happens! Each day is unique. These pages will help you to record your experiences. You may have seen a Dung Beetle laboriously rolling dung across the road; or sunlight catching the leaves; or the miraculous flight of a raptor. When you get back home you will be able to recall and treasure those memories.

The Lion *(Panthera leo)*

Lions are social cats. They often hunt for larger prey, such as zebra, in groups of two or more, as this increases their success rate. (For lion see also page 21).

(1) Lions normally try to get as close as possible to their prey before going in for the kill.

(2) They stalk with their heads low, legs bent, and bodies tense and ready to react. They move only when the prey is not looking in their direction. When they are within 20 - 30 metres, they rush at the herd and try to scatter it in panic.

(3) The other lions in the hunt try to cut off one member of the herd.

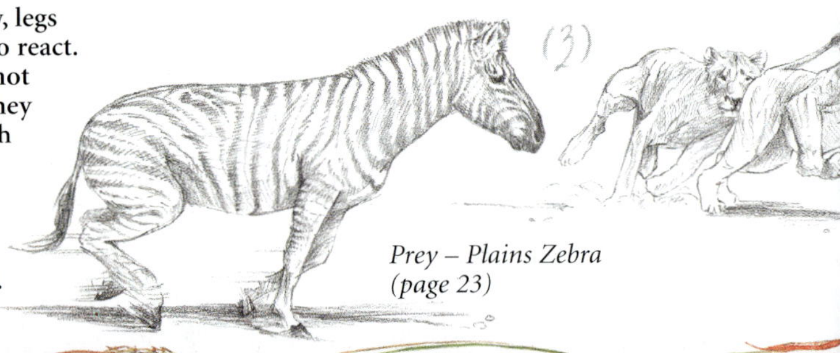

Prey – Plains Zebra (page 23)

(4) The best-positioned lion surges forward and leaps onto the rump or shoulders of the chosen prey, throwing the animal off balance. As soon as the prey falls, it is grabbed by the throat to strangle or suffocate it. Sometimes it bleeds to death. The lions start feeding at the groin where the skin is soft, tearing it open to expose the intestines. The strongest lions feed first, and tear the skin over the back to expose the flesh of the limbs.

(5) If the males hear the lionesses feeding, they rush in, pushing the females off the kill. Females, too, have their fill before allowing cubs to feed. If there is still meat left over after the first "banquet", the pride often stays around to guard it against scavengers. Male lions often hunt on their own when not with the pride.

Gameviewing Journal

The Cheetah *(Acinonyx jubatus)*

Cheetah can be identified by the characteristic tearmarks, and by the fact that their spots are solid, and not arranged in rosettes like those of the leopard. (For cheetah see also page 21).

(1) Cheetah often rest on mounds and fallen trees, from where they locate their prey, using both eyes and ears.

(2 - 3) They are opportunistic predators, and take the most abundant and easily captured animals, often weaker or younger individuals such as wildebeest calves or young impala. They start rushing at the prey from 70 - 100 m away.

(4) They can pursue their prey for about 300 m.

(5) Cheetah are the fastest land mammals on earth, reaching a speed of up to 112 km/h, averaging about 64 km/h. They can therefore outrun any prey, and the faster the fleeing animal runs, the easier it is to knock it off balance.

Prey –
Young impala
(page 24)

(6) The cheetah brings down the prey by striking the rump, thigh or hind legs sideways or downwards with a forepaw, or by simply tripping it. The large dewclaw on the cheetah's front foot often helps to trip an animal.

(7) The prey is grabbed from behind and strangled. It is taken by the throat and dragged to cover before the cheetah starts feeding. The groin is then torn open with the cheek teeth, exposing the muscles of the limbs and back. These and the neck muscles are normally eaten first. If disturbed and chased away by other predators, cheetah do not return to their kills.

Gameviewing Journal

The Leopard *(Panthera pardus)*

Identify leopards by their spots arranged in black rosettes with a yellow-brown centre. Solitary predators, they are more successful when they hunt at night. The main prey is impala, but they also take smaller prey such as Vervet Monkeys and guineafowl. (For leopard see also page 21).

(1) Leopard often lie in wait in dry stream beds, or on well-used paths to waterholes, where they ambush animals that come by. They wait until the prey is very close (about 3 m), then pounce before it has time to react. To kill the prey, the leopard first paralyses it with a bite through the back of the neck that damages the spinal cord.

(2) It then strangles the prey with its powerful jaws. The kill is taken by the neck and dragged away between the leopard's legs. Leopard are very strong, and can lift a carcass of their own weight into a tree.

Prey – impala (F
(page 24)

(3) Prey the size of a large impala can st for more than one meal. It is usually vedged tightly into a fork in a tree with se foliage, about 6 m above the ground. This protects it from vengers and from other carnivores. ok for prey stored in evergreen trees in winter, and in dense eciduous trees along iverbeds in summer.

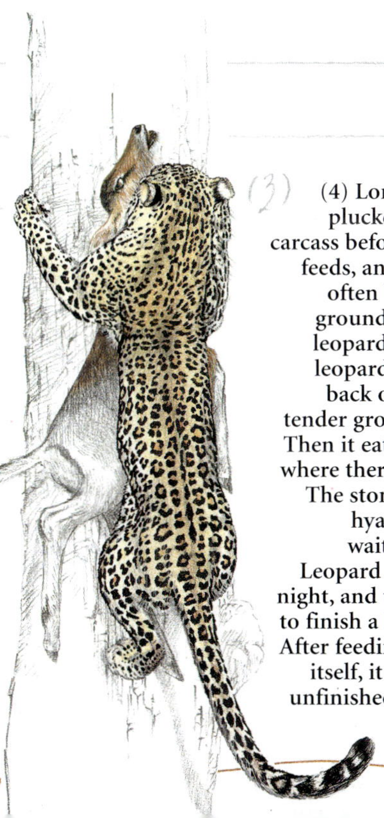

(4) Long hair is plucked from the carcass before the leopard feeds, and bits of hair can often be seen lying on the ground under a tree where a leopard has stored a kill. The leopard starts feeding at the back of the carcass, in the tender groin and anal region. Then it eats the hind-quarter where there is the most flesh. The stomach is left for the hyaenas, which often wait under the tree. Leopard usually feed at night, and take 2 - 3 days to finish a larger carcass. After feeding and cleaning itself, it rests close by, where the unfinished carcass can be watched.

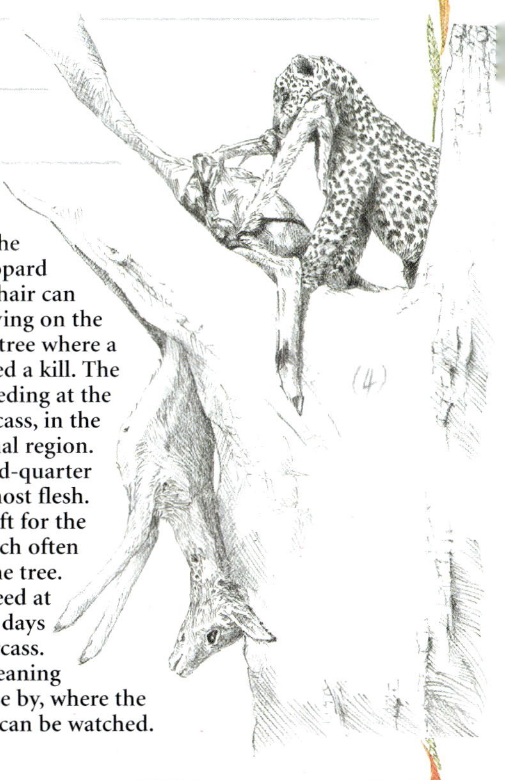

Gameviewing Journal

Wild Dogs *(Lycaon pictus)*

Wild Dogs are among Africa's most endangered mammals, and have been heavily persecuted by humans. They tend to avoid areas with high lion populations, as lions kill both adult dogs and pups. Wild Dogs move over large territories, but stay in one area during mid-winter, when the newborn pups are too small to move. They live in groups of 3 - 30, and after cheetah are the most successful hunters per hunting attempt. (For Wild Dog see also page 20).

(1) Wild Dogs hunt in packs and walk through an area looking for prey. In tall grass the dogs stand up on their hind legs to improve their chance of spotting animals such as impala or wildebeest calves. They chase the first prey they find. One dog starts the rush, with the rest of the pack spreading out over a wide area.

Prey –
Blue Wildebeest calf
(page 23)

(2) The dogs can reach a speed of 64 km/h, and can maintain a speed of 55 km/h for up to 5 km. As soon as the prey animals see the dogs they start to flee, and the hunting pack scatters with the herd. One selected animal is then chased to the point of exhaustion.

(3) The exhausted prey is often held by the lip or muzzle by one dog, and the other dogs disembowel it while it is still standing. It dies within minutes from shock and loss of blood.

(4) The carcass is not dragged or hidden away, as Wild Dogs can defend their prey effectively. They tear large pieces of meat from the carcass and gulp them down. Young puppies are fed back at the den with food regurgitated by all members of the pack.

INDEX

Combretum pods (page 5)

Red-banded Rubber Frog (page 33)